Jamie M. Calise is a veteran law enforcement officer and police administrator. He is currently a police chief in Massachusetts, and for more than two decades, served as a municipal police officer in Rhode Island. An attorney and educator, Calise has extensive experience in public safety administration, patrol operations, investigations, law enforcement accreditation, and police management. He has instructed on several criminal justice topics in police academy and college settings. His courses have included police report writing, criminal procedure, investigations, first-line supervision, legal issues in human resources, and field training.

To Julie, for making this, and so much more possible.

To Mom, for always being you.

Jamie M. Calise

It Did Happen: A Police Officer's Guide to Successful Report Writing

AUSTIN MACAULEY PUBLISHERS®

LONDON * CAMBRIDGE * NEW YORK * SHARJAH

Ordering Information
Quantity sales: Special discounts are available on quantity purchases by corporations, associations, and others. For details, contact the publisher at the address below.

Publisher's Cataloging-in-Publication data
Calise, Jamie M.
It Did Happen: A Police Officer's Guide to Successful Report Writing

ISBN 9798889103240 (Paperback)
ISBN 9798889103257 (ePub e-book)

Library of Congress Control Number: 2023919498

www.austinmacauley.com/us

First Published 2024
Austin Macauley Publishers LLC
40 Wall Street, 33rd Floor, Suite 3302
New York, NY 10005
USA

mail-usa@austinmacauley.com
+1 (646) 5125767

In memory of my grandparents, Frank and Josephine, and my uncle Frank. I am forever grateful for your guidance, love, and support.

Table of Contents

Chapter 1
An Introduction to Police Report Writing

Report writing is one of the most vital responsibilities of a law enforcement officer. As we will discuss in detail in this book, police reports serve many functions in the criminal justice system. Each report provides a window from which the public can view the daily activities of a police agency.

Modern day police departments prioritize transparency and agency accessibility in their efforts to promote the public's trust. Time has shown that successful police departments are those that have gained the confidence of the communities they serve.

Due to ever-advancing technology and better tools for sharing information, many of the inner workings of police departments are now publicly displayed. Common among police agencies is increased social media use and interactive agency websites. Moreover, from twenty-four-hour news coverage to the advent of police oversight committees and civilian review boards, our present-day society meticulously examines the actions of law enforcement personnel. As a result, police reports have taken on new life within the criminal justice field and the importance of clear and effective police reports has never been greater.

Today, the role of a police agency has expanded and officers work in a field that has become increasingly complex and diverse. They are asked to be social workers, mental health professionals, arbitrators, law enforcers, friends, and mentors. Police reports, in a very real sense, have become a direct reflection of an agency's mission and the overall competency of its members.

Broadly speaking, a police report is a written repository of the facts and circumstances learned by an officer during an investigation. Good reports include not only what occurred, but also what the officer did as a result.

At the outset of this book, the reader must appreciate that a police report has the legal endorsement of the issuing officer, as well as the supervisor who approves it. *This is not an insignificant fact.* When police officers submit their reports, they verify that their accounts are truthful, factual, and written without passion or prejudice. Supervisors who then review and approve those reports endorse that the reporting officer's actions were lawful and proper.

As we will discuss in the chapters ahead, police reports document situations that run the gamut. They are not limited to arrests. In fact, there are many non-criminal events that become the topics of police reports. Each day in the United States, a significant number of reports are written to document motor vehicle crash investigations, community policing events, traffic stops, field interviews, civil disturbances, and many other things. These reports are used by many people and for a variety of purposes. Common report audiences include, but are not limited to, other officers, prosecutors, police administrators, insurance company employees, oversight committee members, media personnel, crime victims, and governmental employees. To this end, this book is a good resource for any profession that requires investigative reports as part of its duties.

Reports and the Officers Who Write Them

While a police report details what transpired during an event, they are often a tool used by others to evaluate an officer's *decision-making*. This means that every police report must leave the reader with the assurance that the actions taken by the reporting officer were reasonable under the circumstances. Actions, whether proactive or reactive, are representations of the judgment calls that police officers make.

For purposes of this book, then, let us start with the general premise that *police reports describe the happening of an event and an officer's response to that event*. In essence, every situation an officer confronts dictates the nature of that officer's response. A robbery call may prompt an officer to use physical force, while a lost child call may prompt the officer to utilize a highway message board. In this way, the specific facts of the event pave the road that the officer needs to travel.

Since policing is not an exact science and each new fact introduced has the potential to turn a situation on its head, *sound judgment is a necessity*. In my career, I have learned that decision-making is enhanced when officers are able to identify their legal duties while considering the options available to them. But how does this work? Consider the following general statement:

Duty + Discretion = Decision

This general approach can have broad applicability.

Decisions in a law enforcement context can best be defined as the affirmative steps officers take based on the conclusions they reach. Decisions *must* consider facts and circumstances as they are found. Officers need not have *all* the information related to an event to make a decision. Rather, they just need *sufficient* information. It is a rarity that every piece of information is immediately discernible.

At the same time, officers must be cognizant of their *duties* and the acceptable *discretionary actions* available to them. We know that duties can be legal, policy driven, regulatory, or ethically based. For example, an officer may be bound to act in a certain way when the law dictates an outcome. This is common with domestic violence statutes that mandate a suspect's arrest if probable cause exists. But while duties are generally defined, discretionary actions are not. Instead, discretion necessitates that officers digest the available alternatives. And while the use of discretion, in and of itself, is a decision, it is the officer's ability to choose among viable options that is of importance here.

Minimally, every police report should document the investigating officer's decisions as well as the reasons for those decisions. While we will cover this in greater depth later, we begin with the premise that all investigations are simply *searches for answers*. Invariably, those answers will then generate more questions.

To better appreciate this, let us take, for instance, an officer who is dispatched to investigate whether a vehicle had been vandalized. Think about the following questions and how each may guide the officer's decision-making.

- **Did a crime occur? What if the damage was caused by nature or *unintentionally* by another?**
- **If no crime occurred, is further police action needed?**
- **If a crime did occur, is an investigation needed? What would that entail?**
    - **Observations: What did the officer see or hear?**
    - **Actions: Did the officer search for witnesses? Photograph damage? Seize evidence? Obtain witness statements?**

- **Connections: Did the officer make reasonable inferences from direct or indirect evidence?**
- **What are the next steps?**

This is but a sampling of factors that an officer may need to consider during an investigation. Where this could lead is anyone's guess. For instance, the officer could uncover evidence and arrest the perpetrator. The officer could also reach a dead end and decide to close the case. What if the case took a turn and revealed that the alleged "victim" was attempting to file a false insurance claim?

Regardless of the direction that the investigation takes, the final report must document (1) the facts and circumstances the officer learned during the investigation, (2) the actions the officer took based on those facts and circumstances, and (3) the disposition of the case.

So, Here We Are

Since you are reading this book, I will assume you have either some interest in the criminal justice field or some involvement in law enforcement. You may be a college student, a police academy trainee, an active officer seeking refresher training, or someone who is responsible for writing investigative reports. In order to dive a bit more deeply into some of the nuances of law enforcement report writing, we will touch upon some common procedural topics. A basic familiarity with regularly encountered criminal procedure topics will be helpful as you work your way through this book.

Also, as we progress through different subject areas, it is important for the reader to recognize that the rules or strategies we discuss in this book are *general* ones. They are by no means absolute. We are exploring matters that are very fluid and each investigation depends heavily on the facts and circumstances presented. The result is that exceptions will usually accompany a rule or strategy. In fact, *the only certain rule is that every rule will have an exception.* In policing, there are often different ways to approach an investigation, so the mechanics of narrative writing can vary. The imprecise nature of everyday life requires it. Consequently, the expectation that officers must be adaptable and analytical is very real, especially when the prevalence of situational or legal nuance is so great.

Our focus will not be on the study of grammar or English composition. Instead, we will focus on information gathering and the process of reducing that information into a workable, structured, and comprehensive report. Police officers are trained observers and there is no shortage of information that can be uncovered by an inquisitive investigator. Often, though, the challenge is not just identifying information, but also properly synthesizing it into a clear and organized form. An officer's investigative proficiency, or the connections that exist between pieces of information, will be unknown if information is not properly documented.

Throughout this book, I will use the terms "police report," "report narrative," or some variation thereof, interchangeably. For our purposes, these terms mean the same thing. However, there are additional parts of a police report beyond the basic narrative portion. These commonly include witness statements, hand-written sketches, rights forms, evidence logs, "face" sheets, and a host of other forms. During our examination of police report writing, whenever a new document is introduced, it will be described and discussed.

Lastly, as we consider the various approaches to report writing, you will see that the references made to persons writing police reports will be officers, law enforcement members, or some variation thereof. Although this book is primarily geared towards police reports, it is also applicable to other areas of the criminal justice system. The topics we will cover may be helpful to investigators who work in other state or federal agencies; correctional officers; sheriffs and constables; military members; private investigators; and persons employed in the private security field. Similarly, this book may be beneficial in different educational settings beyond the police academy, such as professional development seminars or secondary or post-secondary courses. In the end, our main goal is to enhance the quality of reports by taking a comprehensive look at the investigative process itself and how it impacts the act of writing.

Where Do We Start?

Police officers require extensive training to survive in the law enforcement world today. Survival, in this sense, means both physical safety and professional durability. Training, when coupled with experience, polishes the lens through which officers view the law enforcement world. Together, training and experience provide them with the best opportunity for success. Each call affords officers with opportunities to refine their professional skills.

Proper training and experience are necessary in policing to help officers develop their own problem-solving roadmap. Instincts are important, but not all instinctive responses are appropriate or lawful in policing. Training helps officers refine their responses to ensure that their actions comport with best practices. As a result, good officers learn to identify clues, make factual connections and reasonable inferences, and act with an open mind. They must become familiar with the law and professional ethics. Much of what officers do each day is based on legal mandates, procedural duties, or policy directives.

While report writing is an integral part of countless professions and job industries, it takes on a special role in the criminal justice world. Officers deal with critical life or death situations and must find the proper balance between public safety and individual liberties. Then, they must be able to articulate their rationale for the decisions they make. Consequently, report writing is an integral part of the police academy curriculum nationwide. It is also frequently part of security training courses, professional development seminars, and college-level criminal justice programs.

You have likely heard the maxim *"if it's not in the report, it didn't happen."* This adage is certainly true from both a practical and legal standpoint. As a practical matter, an officer's failure to document information can hamper the progress of an investigation. For instance, other officers involved in the case may be without knowledge that could be vital in making later factual connections. As a legal matter, an officer's failure to report information is tantamount to that information having not existed in the first place. Consequently, *cases can fail for reasons unrelated to a suspect's guilt.*

If information is material to an investigation – that is to say, it can impact the outcome of the case – then it must be *completely* and *accurately* documented in the police report. Here, quality field notes and the ability to organize information will be of great help. With few exceptions, the idea that less is more does not apply to police reports.

In law enforcement, the stark reality of a poor report is that it can become weaponry used against the issuing officer. At times, the report may also operate as a shield for the defendant. Poor reporting is particularly destructive in those cases that have been pieced together incrementally. Information learned in stages may later yield a comprehensive investigative picture, but most critical deductions rely on the accumulation of small facts. Seasoned police officers know that successful investigations are made by *following the evidence*, since evidence alone is the ultimate navigator. When officers fail to properly document the progression of the case, they do so at their own peril.

Take, for instance, an investigation that resulted in the arrest of a suspect. As part of the prosecutorial process, the associated reports are forwarded to the district attorney's office. Any failure by the officer to document information, however benign it may appear, may open the door to a variety of arguments. The defense may allege officer incompetence or a flawed investigative process. In more extreme cases, the officer who testifies to information absent from the original report may face allegations of impropriety. Defense counsel might argue that the testimony was fabricated, or information was manufactured for a specific purpose. As an example, consider the following scenario:

You are on patrol. As you travel down the road, you see a car swerve into oncoming traffic and nearly collide with another vehicle. You recognize the dangers associated with this type of driving and conduct a traffic stop.

After speaking with the driver, you suspect him to be under the influence of alcohol. You ask him to submit to field sobriety tests to assess his fitness to drive.

Once these tests are concluded, you determine that he is too impaired to safely operate a vehicle and arrest him.

Later, in your report, you document the driver's physical condition. You describe his bloodshot eyes, poor balance, slurred speech, and the distinct odor of an alcoholic beverage on his breath. However, you fail to articulate your reason for stopping the car in the first place.

When you are called to testify, you attempt to explain the violation you observed but are met with a defense objection. The defense attorney confronts you with your police report, and then argues that nowhere in the report is a reference to a traffic offense. What is the ruling?

In this scenario, the case would likely be dismissed. You failed to adequately describe the reasons for your *initial decision* to conduct a traffic stop (i.e., the probable cause for the stop, more on this later). Facts absent from a police report often have the legal effect of them not occurring in the first place. Consequently, a variety of successful legal challenges can be made.

In this case, the missing information would call into question the lawfulness of the stop itself. For instance, if the *initial* stop had no legal justification, any evidence that flowed from it would likely be excluded at trial. This would include your observations of the physical condition of the driver and his failure of the field sobriety tests.

While this example may seem harsh, it occurs frequently in the criminal justice system. Bear in mind that there is a common misconception that criminal trials have the purpose of determining whether a person is *guilty* or *innocent* of a crime. This is not accurate. Under the law, a "not guilty" finding is not synonymous with innocence. *It simply means that the state has failed to prove its case beyond a reasonable doubt.*[1] That is it. In the previous example, the defense attorney was not arguing that the defendant was sober. Instead, the attorney's argument was one of procedure. If the arresting officer lacked probable cause to stop the car, anything the officer learned following the "unlawful" stop becomes inadmissible. This would include the officer's observations of the defendant, the defendant's performance during the field sobriety tests, and so on.

Attacks on police competency, or even worse, police integrity, are increasingly hampering the profession. Most notably, they are impacting the recruitment and retention of qualified staff. For those who are committed to their duties, harsh criticisms can be both galling and disheartening. The lesson here is that fertile defense arguments can be made if police officers seek to testify to information absent from their report. It does not matter if the missing information was simply an oversight.

In today's world, the demand for professionalism in policing means that poor reporting may negatively impact the individual officer, the case itself, or the entire agency. Police officers may face disciplinary measures – up to and including termination – for failing to meet minimum performance standards. Report writing issues can result in evidence suppression, case dismissals,

---

[1] 4 Miss. C. L. Rev. 47 (1983 – 1984), *Not Guilty and Innocent – The Problem Children of Reasonable Doubt.* Vincent Bugliosi.

or other significant legal consequences. In extreme cases, civil liability for the officer and agency can be assessed. Without solid police reports, the true connections between the offense and the offender can easily be destroyed.

We Must Begin with the Criminal Justice Process Itself

In our system of justice, a criminal investigation is the mechanism used to uncover evidence to support a criminal charge. The later prosecution of a defendant, whether through trial, plea bargaining, or some other form of pretrial intervention, determines whether the state has effectively met its burden of proof. As we will discuss in Chapter 3, *probable cause* is the legal threshold necessary to charge a person with a crime. Once a case reaches the prosecution stage, the burden of proof shifts to a higher standard, which is *proof beyond a reasonable doubt*. This standard is always the state's burden to meet.

At the trial stage, if there is ever a reason for a judge or juror to have a reasonable doubt, it is the absence of evidence that connects a defendant to the crime alleged. Picture yourself sitting in the jury box. Would it be unreasonable to ask yourself why, if a fact was so important, it was excluded from the officer's report? If critical information is absent, the burden of proof is a difficult one to meet.

Chapter 2
The Purposes of Police Reports

There are obvious needs for police reports. We know that law enforcement serves a governmental function and involves procedures that can directly impact a person's individual liberties. The best example of this is when a person is arrested and charged with a crime. However, there are also more unapparent reasons for police report writing, and these necessitate a deeper understanding of the *purposes* of police reports. Ultimately, for officers to be successful report writers, it is essential that they grasp not only *how* the process occurs, but also *why* it occurs.

Like many people who must complete reports as part of their employment, police officers must identify their target audience. This, of course, does not mean that a report is only written for a certain person or entity. Nothing could be further from the truth. Police reports, with a few exceptions, are public records that are readily available to anyone who seeks them. Generally, a person can submit a report request to a police agency, pay a small administrative fee, and receive a copy of a report - no questions asked.

When an agency decides to deny access to a report, the denial must be based on a statutory exception and invoked in good faith. Some of the common reasons for withholding reports include open or ongoing investigations; cases involving juvenile arrests or domestic violence; the reasonable belief that information within the report could compromise a person's public safety; and whether release would create an unwarranted invasion of personal privacy. At times, portions of an exempted report may still be released if public information can be segregated from that which is confidential. Other times, departments may redact certain aspects of the case. Most states have some form of monetary punitive measures for agencies that fail to comply with applicable records release statutes.

As you will see, everyday police reports memorialize a wide variety of events. In fact, the number of potential circumstances that require a police report is virtually limitless. Remember that police reports explain the reasoning behind officers' decisions to take official action. Put another way, *police reports document the facts and circumstances that resulted in officers exercising their legally vested authority.* Here are some of the common functions of police reports:

- **To document crimes, arrests, investigations, and events requiring a police officer's response.**
- **To document motor vehicle crash investigations.**
- **To demonstrate compliance with certain legal mandates, such as statistical information compiled by the FBI.**
- **To document civil complaints when police presence is needed or recommended.**
- **To provide a mechanism for recording information aimed at ensuring fairness in the criminal justice system.**
- **To give follow-up investigators a frame of reference.**
- **To inform members of public bodies or police leaders when making policy decisions.**
- **To create historical records for crime analysis that can be used operationally, administratively, or legislatively.**

Good police reports answer key questions. At a minimum, even when some answers are unknown, reports should describe the steps that officers took as they attempted to answer those questions. While simplistic, this view of reporting offers a keen insight into a fundamental priority of police officers – they *must* problem-solve and locate information as part of their daily responsibilities. Remember, police officers are trained observers who are vested with the duty of enforcing the law, keeping the peace, and protecting the public. Consequently, officers are required to *investigate* incidents, not just *report* on those incidents. I have heard it best described as "an officer is not a spectator of the game, but rather a participant."

The short answer, then, to the question of "Why do we write police reports?" is that *police officers must document information for others to read.* Whether that information will be used in a criminal trial, in a hearing before a state agency, or by an insurance company to make a liability determination, the information contained within a report will be utilized. The more clearly documented the information is, the more effective and useful it will be.

Who Reads Police Reports?

There is no question that organizational transparency is a necessity in today's public safety world. It is common to see police reports sought by:

- **Police personnel (i.e., executives, commanders, administrators, supervisors, detectives, officers).**
- **Attorneys (prosecutors, defense counsel, civil litigators).**
- **Crime victims and victims' advocates.**
- **Courts.**
- **Insurance companies.**
- **Media personnel.**
- **Citizens.**
- **Civic groups and organized bodies (public or private).**
- **Town or city leaders.**
- **Governing bodies (i.e., city councils, town councils, or select boards).**
- **Members of elected or appointed government boards.**
- **State or federal agencies.**
- **Members of the legislature.**

While dependent on the case, it is likely that every police report will at least be read by some of those referenced above. If a case involves a serious incident or is a matter of significant public interest, it will likely be read by most of them.

Let us consider a basic example:

Officer Adams investigates a theft and completes a police report. She concludes that the victim's purse was stolen from a gym locker. As part of her investigation, Officer Adams reviews surveillance footage and speaks with several witnesses. She determines that the theft was consistent with other recent thefts that have occurred within her district. At the end of her patrol shift, she forwards the case to the detective unit for follow-up measures.

In her narrative, Officer Adams must describe each of her investigative steps and her preliminary findings. For instance, Officer Adams' report should note who had been interviewed, which addresses she visited, whether she had identified or seized any evidence, and so on. The level of detail she uses will help with the next stages of the investigation. The detectives may use the information to (1) search for more victims or witnesses, (2) re-interview those already identified, (3) process any seized evidence, or (4) if probable cause is established, issue an arrest warrant.

Regardless of the case's outcome, though, Officer Adams' police report will contribute to her agency's ability to identify crime trends. The details she includes may prove useful in identifying (1) crime hotspots, (2) specific timeframes of increased criminal activity, or (3) the modus operandi used by the perpetrators. If any crime trends are determined, her agency may publicly share information, such as a social media post, or it may send a bulletin for distribution at police roll call. Similarly, any noted crime trends may result in the use of targeted patrols or specialized assignments. The lesson here is that historical information can be used in a variety of ways, and it remains one of the best tools for law enforcement.

Anything Else?

Along with the functional uses of historical information, there are also valuable byproducts. For instance, crime analysis results can be utilized by policymakers to determine personnel needs or to make operational recommendations. If a police chief is seeking to increase an agency's staffing complement, an examination of call volume will be important.

If you are a new police officer, you are probably surprised by the sheer volume of paperwork generated from everyday police work. Police reports include face sheets, statement forms, rights forms, evidence logs, property tracking numbers, photographs, scanned images, certifications, victim assessments, sworn affidavits, notarized documents, and so on. Unfortunately, with the many administrative and procedural requirements that accompany police investigations, information can be overlooked. And, as previously noted, the negative impact of missed information can be substantial. *Too often, the quality of a police report is judged not on its contents, but rather on what it lacked.* Diligence provides officers with firm footing to demonstrate their competence and professionalism.

A Note on Police Calls in General

While police officers will respond to many different situations, not every call they encounter will require an "official" report. For the purposes of this book, we will define an "official" police report as a document, created by an agency member in the ordinary course of their daily activities, that includes a unique report number, a face sheet, and a report narrative. The face sheet and report narrative will be discussed in more detail later.

When a call is initially received by a public safety dispatcher, it is entered into a computerized system, commonly referred to as a computer-aided dispatch (CAD) system. The CAD system is part of the police department's overall records management system (RMS). While dispatch policies for departments will vary, it is fair to say that not every phone call to a police department requires that an officer respond somewhere. Many times, members of the public call the police department with general requests, such as to obtain a copy of a police report.

Every law enforcement agency has some form of an RMS or CAD system to log and manage information. Aside from general police activities, these systems house data related to scheduling, training, policy matters, internal complaints, and a host of other administrative functions.

When a department receives a call that requires a police officer's response, there is a permanent record of that call logged within the department's CAD system. While it may sound like a misnomer, police "calls" can also include those instances when an officer performs some type of self-initiated activity, such as a traffic stop or a property check. Moreover, police calls may originate from other agencies, such as when officers receive requests to locate people or issue a protective order. A CAD system is designed to account for all agency activity, resulting in a permanent record of activity.

CAD information is relatively detailed, even when it is not associated with a police report. It is often used to mine information, identify call trends, or determine increases or decreases in call volume. CAD entries typically include contact information and descriptions of people and property, resulting in ongoing historical updates. In this way, CAD systems can promote both officer safety and data accuracy.

In general, a CAD entry includes:

- **The date and time of the call.**
- **The location of the call (i.e., address).**
- **The reason(s) for the call (i.e., burglary alarm, barking dog).**
- **The person reporting the call.**
- **The officer dispatched to the call.**
- **The officer's findings.**
- **The call's disposition (i.e., complaint unfounded, peace restored).**

Specific requirements for "official" report-taking are dictated by each department's internal policies, state statutes (i.e., mandatory domestic violence reporting), and of course, the officer's common sense. Newer officers, when confronted with unusual or unfamiliar events, may question whether it is appropriate to take a police report. Supervisors will provide officers with guidance in these situations, especially as they become familiar with their agency's requirements. Sometimes, the most fitting response for a new officer is, "When in doubt, take a report."

Importantly, though, officers must remember that even when no "official" police report is required, the call will still be detailed in the agency's CAD system. This entry will include a disposition that explains how the call was resolved. Although the entry may be a limited synopsis, such as "subjects were dispersed" or "the roadway is clear," it will provide the reader with the conclusory information learned during an investigation (criminal or otherwise). To introduce the reader to how this looks in practice, consider the following basic scenario:

Officer Adams is dispatched to the intersection of Elm Street and First Avenue for the report of children playing baseball in the roadway. The reporting person stated that the children were obstructing traffic.

Officer Adams responds to the area. He observes that there is no one around but decides to monitor the intersection for several minutes. During that time, no one appears. Officer Adams determines that the call was "unfounded" since he could not verify that children were creating a traffic hazard.

In this scenario, Officer Adams does not need to take an "official" police report. The CAD entry alone will document the date and time of the call, the address, the reporting person, the nature of the complaint, Officer Adams' personal observations, and a final disposition. With no crimes involved and no hazards present, a full police report was not warranted. Instead, a CAD entry alone was sufficient.

Imagine, instead, that in the above scenario, when Officer Adams arrives on scene, he sees several children in the area and observes one of them break the window of a parked car. Does this fact change how Officer Adams should handle the call? If your answer is "yes," then you are correct. Let's take a look.

With the addition of damaged property, there is now fertile ground for Officer Adams to take an official report. Vandalism is a crime, so Officer Adams would need to conduct a criminal investigation, which would start by him notifying the vehicle's owner and attempting to identify the suspect. Officer Adams would want to determine whether the owner wished to file a complaint and if probable cause existed to make an arrest. He would also likely document the damage with photographs, question witnesses, determine the value of the loss, and so on.

Unfortunately, there is not an all-encompassing list that defines when an official police report *is* required. Instead, officers should use reason and common sense, and they must consider local rules, applicable state laws, and their agency's policies. They must also be mindful that the cases they encounter will frequently differ in severity, and there are a range of possibilities along the criminal justice spectrum. Some cases will undoubtedly require an official police report, such as a murder investigation, and other cases will require judgment calls, such as a noise complaint. As cases shift from one end of the spectrum to the other, officers must learn when and how to use their discretion.

Below are some general questions that officers can ask themselves when considering whether a police report is warranted. These questions are meant to provide some general guidance, and officers are encouraged to look to their agency's policies for specific direction.

- **Is the officer *statutorily obligated* to complete a report? This is common with domestic violence laws, elder abuse and neglect cases, child abuse cases, and hate crimes.**

- Does the *agency itself require* officers to complete a report by policy or general order?
- Did the officer *arrest* or *detain* a person? If so, the officer must clearly articulate the legal basis for doing so, such as probable cause or the presence of a Fourth Amendment exception.
- Did the officer *search* a person or property? Like arrests and detentions, searches must be based on probable cause or an exception to the warrant requirement.
- Does the officer *need to investigate*? For example, was the officer investigating a crime, or attempting to determine if a crime occurred?
- Does the officer need to involve *another state* or *federal agency* in the investigation? If so, the officer must document specific information related to a mutual aid request. In some cases, the requested agency may take jurisdiction over the investigation itself.
- Does the victim of a crime or incident need to document an event for *insurance purposes*? This is common when insured items are stolen, such as motor vehicles, credit cards, or jewelry.
- Does the agency have a policy that requires a report as a means of *identifying crime trends* or *patterns*? This is typically agency specific, but crime statistics are also reported to the federal government for national crime reporting through NIBRS and UCR.

These questions offer a good starting point for considering whether an official police report is appropriate. As you might imagine, circumstances do not always fit neatly into a particular category, and an officer's use of discretion is common and necessary. Veteran officers will tell you that police encounter circumstances that are atypical and not easily foreseeable. It will not be long before new officers hear someone comment "you cannot make this stuff up." As part of most department training programs, officers must read and digest their agency's field operations manual, which outlines its approach to reporting.

More on Police "Calls for Service"

Requests for the police come in a variety of forms. Not all calls are an emergency, and as previously discussed, some may be initiated by on-duty officers or another agency. As a matter of public duty, officers must respond to the requests that they receive. They are generally without the authority to select which calls will be answered. If a call is later deemed to be unsubstantiated or unfounded, that finding will be based on the officer's investigation.

Some of the common ways that police departments receive "calls for service" include the following:

- **<u>Walk-in calls</u>. This is when a person visits the police station to make a report or file a complaint.**
- **<u>Telephone requests</u>. These include emergency calls, non-emergency calls, and those relayed from 911 service centers.**
- **<u>Mutual aid agency requests</u>. Outside agencies frequently seek the assistance of local police departments. Some of the more common requests include making official notifications, serving orders or other forms of court process, or attempting to locate wanted subjects.**
- **<u>Online requests</u>. Many police departments have online fillable forms and other interactive media on their websites. Calls may be generated from a person's online inquiry or complaint.**
- **<u>Follow-up investigations from previous calls</u>. Each department has its own specific policies for investigations, but most require some form of case follow-up. Typical examples are searches for evidence, area canvasses, video retrieval, and the issuance of preservation letters.**

Once a call is received, an officer will be dispatched. The responding officer is then tasked with taking appropriate investigative steps and, when required, completing a police report. Let's take a closer look at how that process occurs.

Getting Started

No two calls are alike, and the complexity of each case will vary. In every instance, officers must act reasonably in light of the circumstances. This means they must recognize when additional resources are preferable or when quick action is necessary. They must also know how to document the stages of a case in a clear and effective way. This can be especially challenging because *the ability to comprehend an event is vastly different from being able to describe it*. One sign that a report is effectively written is that the reader feels as if they are in the officer's shoes.

During investigations, officers acquire information in different ways. They may witness events firsthand or they may receive information through other means. While seemingly minor, this is an important point. There are fundamental evidentiary differences between direct and indirect evidence. Direct evidence generally does not require that the officer make an inference or circumstantial connection to establish a relevant fact, while indirect evidence does. For instance, an officer may personally witness a traffic crash (direct evidence), or may follow a trail of automotive fluid from the scene to a damaged vehicle (indirect evidence). In the latter case, the officer would not have personally witnessed the accident, but would be able to make a reasonable inference that a particular vehicle was involved in the crash.

It is the norm that recruits undergo extensive coursework during the police academy. The result is that trained officers understand the tactics, practices, and procedures discussed within police reports. If a layperson reading those same reports has not undergone specialized training, the reasoning behind each critical decision may not be immediately obvious. In this way, officers must remain mindful that their individual judgments are revealed in their reports, so their sensibility and judiciousness must be clearly articulated.

So, what does a well-written police report look like? Unfortunately, there is no easy answer to this question because no "one size fits all" formula exists. For starters, though, a well-written police report provides answers to the fundamental questions of "who, what, where, when, why, and how." Doing so explains what the officer learned and did with that information. The final report should lead the reader to the irresistible conclusion that the officer's actions were reasonable under the circumstances.

This is not to say that every fundamental investigative question must be answered. This is not possible. Remember that the very nature of an officer's investigation involves the search for information. The key is accurately documenting *what is known, what is unknown, and what steps can or should be taken to find information*. This way, the officer either describes what has been determined or at least explains its absence. When possible, the report could include future steps that can be taken to find the answers.

For instance, let's say an officer responded to a hit and run accident. The victim could not determine the make, model, or registration plate of the suspect's vehicle, but she observed a red SUV strike her car and flee the scene. Here, the officer can document this limited information while noting that the specific vehicle has not yet been identified. The officer may include later investigative steps, such as a search for witnesses or a review of any surveillance cameras facing the area of the crash. This will help to create a better police report.

Although officers will frequently deal with "routine" situations, such as petty criminal offenses and traffic enforcement, they will also respond to incidents that rapidly evolve, increase in complexity, and involve other law enforcement personnel. Criminality has no boundaries and does not consider an officer's experience level. A lesser experienced officer is just as likely to be dispatched to a complex call as an experienced one.

So, in the report writing sense, preparation for an investigation and the ability to organize information begins before an officer even gets to the scene of the call. For example, imagine that you are the officer in the following scenario:

You receive a call to respond to a robbery in progress. The dispatcher tells you that the panic alarm was set off at XYZ Convenience Store.

Before you arrive, you receive updates from the dispatcher. You are told that there was a witness outside of the store, and he observed a suspect wearing a ski mask run from the store with a black handgun in his right hand. The suspect was seen entering a blue sedan that had several bumper stickers on the rear trunk. The witness believed that the suspect was alone but could not provide the registration plate or vehicle's make. The car reportedly headed north on Main Avenue.

Would you agree that before you can write a detailed report about this case, you would first need to know how to handle the call? Where is a good place to start?

Police officers must always consider their personal safety and the safety of others. At the same time, they must use proper tactics and employ good investigative techniques. And they must be mindful of potential outcomes. If you were the responding officer, you may ask yourself:

- **Should I respond with my lights and siren activated to get there quickly, or should I shut down my emergency equipment to maintain the element of surprise?**
- **Should I respond directly to the store, or should I divert and search for the suspect's vehicle?**
- **Was the victim of the robbery injured?**
- **How many people witnessed the robbery?**
- **How many back-up officers are needed to assist in the investigation?**

You can see that a wide range of variables would need to be considered in this case. As a law enforcement professional, your knowledge and skillset becomes a critical aspect of the report writing process. This is so because your actions – later documented in the report – must comport with best practices and how you were trained. Using this fact pattern, let us go a few steps further.

You respond directly to the store to verify that no one is injured and speak with the victim and witness. You conclude that the best chance of solving the case is by relaying more detailed information to surrounding officers.

Officers who encounter multi-faceted situations like this one must be able to "think on their feet". For those who are new to the field, multitasking can be a challenging aspect of policing, especially during high stress incidents. In fact, an officer's ability to handle several tasks concurrently is a critical assessment area during field training.

Although demanding, these types of events provide fertile ground for officers to hone their policing skills. In our robbery example, as the first officer, you are presented with many considerations before even arriving at the scene. This is where organizational skills and foresight take center stage. Experience teaches that *while it is important to envision future tasks, it is just as important to prioritize them.*

In this instance, how would your response change if you learned that the suspect's flight from the scene caused a traffic accident? What if the cashier had been seriously injured during the robbery? If someone was injured at the scene, how would you render aid? How would you protect the crime scene from contamination? What resources will be available to you?

Moving forward with our example:

You arrive on scene and learn that the suspect entered the store wearing a red wool facemask. He approached the front counter and demanded money while simultaneously pulling a black handgun from his waistband. The victim reported that the suspect had a deep voice and was wearing a Denver Broncos sweatshirt. Once he received a handful of cash, he ran out of the store.

Although the store is equipped with security cameras, you learn they were turned off. You also learn that besides the victim and witness, there was no one else in the store and no one was injured. You collect written statements from them.

Approximately one hour later, Officer Adams from a neighboring jurisdiction stops a blue vehicle and the driver matches the suspect's description. The officer determines that the driver's criminal record consists of several arrests for theft and drug possession. When questioned, the suspect quickly admits to the robbery.

So, case closed, right? No. Surprisingly, your work has just begun. In this instance, you have a substantial amount of information to document in your police report. For starters, the crime of robbery is a serious offense and you conducted much of the investigation on your own. Your police report must include the chronological facts you learned during your investigation since these helped you chart your investigative route. Remember that any investigation, criminal or otherwise, generally builds upon earlier steps. Importantly, in this example, the findings you sent to the neighboring agency formed the *legal* basis for Officer Adams' stop.

If your report lacked any critical information, it could undermine, or even worse, invalidate the legality of Officer Adams' traffic stop. Criminal defense attorneys will search for procedural errors in an investigation since these types of errors provide fertile ground for case dismissals, especially in the early stages of a prosecution. Many times, dismissals result from legal technicalities, not factual circumstances.

For instance, in this scenario, if the defense attorney could demonstrate that the defendant had not been advised of his Miranda warnings before admitting to the robbery, then the subsequent inculpatory statements could be suppressed. This drastic consequence is based on the application of the exclusionary rule, whereby the statement would be considered invalid – even if truthful –if it was illegally obtained. While we will discuss this rule in more detail in Chapter 3, suffice it to say that procedural violations can be catastrophic to a case, especially when they involve constitutional safeguards.

But How Do We Know What Is "Critical" for a Police Report?

The answer to this question lies in identifying information that is material to a case. Although this may seem imprecise, materiality becomes clearer as an officer gains experience. Each call and each investigation contribute to an officer's ever-increasing knowledge base. Broadly speaking, material information is information that is reasonably related to a fact or inference that is of consequence to a case. Okay, but what does *that* mean?

Using the robbery example, think about the pieces of information that would have some bearing on the case. For instance, it would be entirely logical for you to include the amount of money stolen when you write your police report. This could provide corroborating evidence if the defendant is later found with the same amount of money or with the specific denominations taken. Likewise, it would have bearing on the specific criminal charge, since the robbery was completed, not just attempted. Moreover, it could support the suspect's motive since there is correlation between theft and drug use. On the contrary, it would not be important for you to document what the victim had for breakfast the day before. That information would not be reasonably related to the case and would have no bearing on the investigation.

Police supervisors and veteran officers are excellent resources, especially when you are involved in a complex case, or if you are operating in new territory. And always remember to think critically and ask questions. You will quickly learn that adaptability and strategic thinking are imperative for success in the law enforcement field. While it is not required that you have the answer to every question you face, you should at least know where to find it.

General Report Classifications

When officers take a police report, they must classify that report into the appropriate category. The most common report categories are:

- **Case reports (sometimes called crime, incident, or offense reports).**
- **Crash (or accident) reports.**
- **Arrest reports.**
- **Field interview reports.**

The above categories are generally considered operational reports. In essence, operational reports are those that deal with the daily workload of an agency. Your department will dictate the types of reports you are responsible for, and we will cover these general categories in more detail later.

Summary

Police reports serve a variety of functions. Whether a report is sought by media personnel, an insurance company, a detective, or a crime victim, its uses are endless. In today's evolving law enforcement world, reports are more than a mere prosecutorial tool or investigative aid. They frequently serve an agency planning function through crime analysis and provide historical information for forecasting operational priorities. Reports can be the first line of defense in a civil lawsuit or may provide necessary historical data to reallocate resources. Irrespective of a report's particular use, though, officers will be well-served by recognizing the far-reaching impacts of their written work.

Chapter 3
Criminal and Non-Criminal Investigations

In this chapter, we will explore the fundamentals of law enforcement investigations. One of the main responsibilities entrusted to police officers is to investigate criminal activity. A combination of good instinct and sound training will be of benefit here. However, beyond criminal cases, officers commonly deal with a wide range of non-criminal events or civil matters. Oftentimes, determining whether a case is criminal or civil only occurs after the officer has conducted some type of inquiry.

Each day, police officers encounter situations that run the gamut. These may involve serious matters, complex circumstances, or nuances that require innovation on the part of the officer. Advances in technology, calls for social justice, and evolving societal norms are but a few examples of conditions that have prompted agencies to formulate varied approaches to policing. While this book is not a policy document, it is helpful for the reader to recognize the transitional nature of policing and its impact on those who serve on the front lines.

In addition to their enforcement duties, officers respond to calls where they must serve as mediators, social workers, and problem solvers. For those events that require an official police report, officers must be able to effectively document the circumstances they encounter. Reports should include the cause of the event (if known) and whether or not follow-up action is required. Even if a police report is not necessarily *required*, there are many instances when a report is *recommended.* It is a commonly accepted aspect of public safety that reports are invaluable tools down the road. This, then, begs the question, "How do you know when a police report *must* be taken or, at a minimum, *should* be taken?"

The first answer to this question, of course, is that a police report must be taken when it is *mandated*. This can be via statute, such as motor vehicle crash reports or cases involving domestic violence. Other times, reports may be required by agency policy, such as incidents involving local bylaw violations or matters impacting protected classes of people. At a minimum, officers will learn the types of reports that are mandatory during their police academy training or while they are assigned to their department's field training program.

The second answer to this question is less certain since there is no exact science to gauge when a non-mandatory police report *should* be completed. Rather, it often becomes a judgment call. Since this represents a gray area for law enforcement, it is incumbent on officers to think critically about the circumstances they encounter. For instance, it is obvious that an officer must write a report to document an arrest, but the need for a report is not so obvious when an officer handles a dispute over a property line. In my experience, many civil situations that have the potential to later erupt into a more volatile encounter are ripe for "official" reporting. Here, patrol supervisors become a crucial resource for new officers. Supervisors introduce new officers to the policing field through the policies and procedures of the agency, but also guide them through the twists and turns of everyday shift work.

Years ago, a police academy instructor, who also served as a patrol supervisor, used to begin his course by pulling a pen from his shirt pocket and describing it as an officer's most important weapon. While symbolic, it has a ring of truth. Reports are a snapshot in time that go beyond the officer's career, changing administrations, and legal evolution.

Let's look at a specific call and then consider whether a police report is warranted.

You are dispatched to 123 Main Street to check on "Tom", an elderly male who lives alone. Tom has not been heard from in two days by his daughter. She describes this as unusual.

Tom reportedly suffers from some medical issues. When you ring the doorbell, you get no response. You check the exterior of the house, and all of the windows and doors are closed and locked. You call the local fire department to see if Tom had been transported to a medical facility during the previous two days. They have no record of such a call.

You determine that Tom could have fallen or suffered a serious medical event and decide to enter the home. In doing so, you force your way in by breaking the door. Once inside, you learn that Tom is on vacation with a friend.

Should you take a report? Why or why not?

In this example, although there were a series of investigative steps, there was no crime involved. The call ultimately had a positive outcome since Tom was confirmed to be safe. While the door to Tom's home was damaged, your actions were taken in good faith and were reasonable under the circumstances. However, there was damage to the door and Tom will likely need to make a claim with the city's insurer. Here, a police report would be recommended since it would (1) provide a detailed account of the event and (2) provide you with the opportunity to explain why your actions were warranted.

This scenario shows how police reports become a tool for officers to describe situations *as they encountered them*. Officers must often act quickly without the benefit of time to deliberate. While hindsight provides an opportunity to consider alternatives, officers are often left without that luxury.

Let us consider another example that deals with a common civil issue encountered by police officers – repossession. In this example, think about how you would handle this incident. If you are already a sworn law enforcement officer, think about how your department's policies and procedures would guide you.

Two employees of a repossession company have requested police assistance in recovering a vehicle. They report that the lessee failed to make several payments and the bank issued a repossession order.

Even though repossessions are civil matters, you know they can trigger conflict. At the same time, you recognize that your authority is generally limited to a peacekeeping role. If the lessee resists, or if the vehicle is parked in a private protected area, then the repossessor must retreat.

What happens if the repossessor attempts to gain entry into the lessee's garage? How about if the lessee and repossessors become involved in a verbal argument or physical altercation?

A call such as this would be a good candidate for a police report, especially if the vehicle was ultimately repossessed or if there was an escalation between the people involved. On the contrary, a formal report may not be required if there was no response at the address and no vehicle transfer took place.

New officers quickly learn that *the only predictable aspect of policing is its unpredictability*. In many situations, when tempers flare, ordinary events can transform from calm to chaos in an instant. Officers must always be mindful that the line between civil and criminal events can quickly be crossed.

The basic tenets of an investigation apply to both criminal and non-criminal cases. One of your primary roles as a law enforcement officer is to uncover information and find a solution. I say solution here specifically because a solution differs from a resolution. Frequently, officers are called to quell matters where only temporary solutions can be provided. In many instances, legal measures beyond a police officer's authority must be taken before an actual resolution can be achieved. Examples of this are child custody matters or property line disputes that require judicial findings.

Procedurally, an officer's approach to a civil matter may differ – for instance, a witness in a civil case need not be advised of Miranda warnings. However, many of the questions that the officer asks will be the same. Similarly, in a civil matter, the officer might wish to note specific observations, such as a person's mental state or overall demeanor.

For every shift, officers must be prepared to encounter latent circumstances. They will be met with investigative obstacles, and information may be indiscernible or elusive. Remember that officers should seek to answer those core investigative questions of "who, what, where, when, why, and how" during their investigations. If a civil matter requires some examination, the steps will generally be the same.

Importantly, while police officers "take reports" in the course of their duties, they are more than just "report takers." Police officers are *trained investigators*. A critical eye is one of the most vital qualities of the successful officer. Lack of investigative diligence can lead to failed cases, and officers being "spoon-fed" information. Instead, officers must systematically probe for the truth, wherever it may reside.

The ABCs of Effective Reports

Whether a case is criminal or civil, police reports must be *articulate, balanced,* and *comprehensive.* Articulate means that the report must be clear and unambiguous. Balanced refers to the objectivity required of police action. And a comprehensive report is one that is complete, with sufficient detail to describe how each investigative question was answered.

Regardless of the circumstances of a particular case, a thorough investigation is one that consists of an officer's search for *facts* and the *reasonable inferences* that flow from those facts. This is a truism in law enforcement and the primary compass needed to find an effective investigative path. For instance, if an officer responds to a car crash and observes an opened beer bottle in one of the vehicles, what can the officer factually report? What can be inferred? Factually, the officer can note the bottle's presence in the vehicle. The inference, however, could be that the driver may have been operating under the influence of liquor, and additional investigation is necessary. As a result, the officer must consider the following possibilities:

- **Does the driver show signs of alcohol impairment, such as slurred speech, poor balance, or bloodshot eyes?**
- **Was the beer consumed at another time? Even though driving with an open container of an alcoholic beverage is unlawful, it is not the same offense as driving under the influence.**
- **Did the driver open the bottle of beer after the crash? In this way, consumption would have had no impact on the crash itself.**

The point here is that there is a big difference between the presence of a beer bottle (a fact), and the driver operating under the influence at the time of the crash (a reasonable inference). Each of the officer's observations will then influence the investigative step that follows. The officer may decide to ask the driver direct questions or request that the driver submit to field sobriety testing. If, say, the driver is unable to pass the field sobriety tests, then the officer has established an additional fact (failed tests) and another reasonable inference that the driver's failure was due to intoxication.

Investigations can ebb and flow and may lead to differing outcomes. Officers can identify inculpatory evidence, which suggests a person's involvement in a crime and helps narrow the focus of the case. Other times, officers may locate exculpatory evidence that demonstrates a person's innocence. Both are critically important.

This last point is a very important one. Police officers take an oath to uphold the Constitution of the United States. This necessarily means that *justice must be the officer's top priority*. Justice can be achieved through a defendant's conviction, but it may also be accomplished when an officer uncovers evidence that exonerates a person. The American system of justice abhors wrongful convictions, since a criminal finding can result in a person's loss of liberty, either temporarily or permanently. As a check and balance, the criminal justice system has multiple procedural and substantive mechanisms that test the lawfulness and strength of a criminal case. In policing, the officer's ultimate investigative goal is simply to find the truth.

Successful cases require investigative competence. Members of law enforcement must make good decisions and employ sound reasoning. However, successful cases *also* require good police reports. There is simply no alternative. If an officer conducts an exceptional investigation, but submits a shoddy police report, the case will likely fail. This is how the system is constructed. It must test the strength of cases, and to withstand scrutiny, cases must be handled properly. This necessarily includes accurately and comprehensively documenting the stages of an investigation in a balanced way.

Bear in mind that strong cases and successful cases are not synonymous. When they are challenged, criminal cases may fail on procedural aspects, regardless of the case's merits. At that time, any cracks in the foundation will likely be exposed. For instance, while a suspect's confession may be compelling, if it was obtained in violation of *Miranda*, it will be of no use. More on this in Chapter 7.

At its core, a conviction in the criminal justice system hinges on the state or government meeting its legal burden of proof. In a criminal case, that burden is defined as proof beyond a reasonable doubt, a hefty threshold to meet. The American system of justice does not require that defendants prove their innocence. Instead, for defendants to avoid conviction, they need only show that the state has failed to meet its requisite burden.

Procedural errors, even minor ones, may result in legal technicalities that can be destructive to the outcome of a case. When officers fail to meet procedural obligations – or when they fail to document how those obligations were met –cases can falter. Our general democratic principles view liberty as a vital fundamental right not to be taken away lightly. Sir William Blackstone famously said that "[i]t is better that ten guilty persons escape than that one innocent suffers." Beyond outright dismissals, though, unsuccessful cases can result in civil liability for the agency, the jurisdiction, and the individual officer.

The Probable Cause Standard

As is taught in police academies, criminal procedure courses, and other law enforcement forums nationwide, the necessary threshold for arresting a criminal defendant, or conducting a search of a person or place, is probable cause. This term is found within the Fourth Amendment to the United States Constitution whereby it is stated that:

The right of the people to be secure in their persons, houses, papers, and effects, against unreasonable searches and seizures, shall not be violated, and no Warrants shall issue, but upon probable cause, supported by Oath or affirmation, and particularly describing the place to be searched, and the persons or things to be seized.

While the concept of probable cause does not lend itself to being easily defined, the Supreme Court has provided that:

In dealing with probable cause...as the very name implies, we deal with probabilities. These are not technical; they are the factual and practical considerations of everyday life on which reasonable and prudent [officers], not legal technicians, act. The standard of proof is accordingly correlative to what must be proved. 'The substance of all the definitions' of probable cause 'is a reasonable ground for belief of guilt.' See Brinegar v. United States, 338 U.S. 160 (1949) (internal citations omitted).

It is quite easy to get mired in lengthy legal definitions and technical language when studying the probable cause standard. And while the above court discussion is helpful, it still begs the practical question of "What is it?" In my experience, a broad understanding of probable cause can be reached through repetition and exposure. In other words, broadened experience leads to a broader understanding of probable cause.

On the flipside, officers who do not fully understand the probable cause standard will struggle to document it in their narrative. Put bluntly, those who do not recognize the individual factors that support the basis of their actions, or who fail to include those factors when they do recognize them, will most certainly write substandard reports. Remember that "missing" information is the functional equivalent of that information not existing in the first place. Therefore, the adage "If it is not in the report, it didn't happen" *has stood the test of time for a reason*. Officers must do their best to avoid being caught in the crosshairs of appearing to lack either knowledge or diligence. They cannot effectively function without comprehending the probable cause standard and how that legal standard looks in practice.

A review of some court cases where probable cause was examined can be helpful. Several years back, the Massachusetts Supreme Judicial Court considered probable cause in terms of an officer's authority to make an arrest, and its discussion summarized the standard when it held:

Probable cause to arrest 'requires more than mere suspicion but something less than evidence sufficient to warrant a conviction. The evidence…must consist of reasonably trustworthy information sufficient to warrant a reasonable or prudent person in believing that the defendant has committed the offense. Commonwealth v. Roman, 609 N.E.2d 1217, 1218 (1993) (internal citations omitted).

Still, theoretical or cerebral exercises are only helpful in setting the stage. They do not ensure a successful production. Officers have an affirmative duty to move beyond simply *defining* probable cause and work towards *understanding* it. It is not enough to say, "I know it when I see it." Repetition is needed. Every time an officer works on a case where probable cause is established, that officer increases his or her familiarization with the standard through representative examples. They get to see when evidence is deemed sufficient and when it is not.

Consider the following. Do the facts alone represent sufficient probable cause to make an arrest or conduct a search? If so, why? If not, what information do you think is missing?

- **You detect the odor of an alcoholic beverage coming from the interior of a car you just stopped.**
- **You see a man running from the scene of a fight, and his shirt is torn.**
- **You check on a tripped house alarm. Although the doors and windows are locked, you see a person lying unconscious on the floor.**
- **You respond to the report of a female walking on a public sidewalk with a rifle strung over her shoulder. The jurisdiction allows for the open carry of weapons.**

It is unmistakable that the criminal justice system rejects the validity of arrests or searches that lack probable cause. All it takes is a glance at the daily news or a review of the court decisions that have shaped present day criminal procedure. This underscores the point that the justice system abhors overreaching by law enforcement, especially in instances when a person's personal liberties are at stake. The mere absence of *articulated* probable cause can render a case invalid. In this way, a suspect's actual involvement in a crime – seemingly the most relevant consideration – can become secondary. Courts take the position that *for the law to be respected, the legal process of enforcing it must be scrupulously followed.*

The Exclusionary Rule Summarized

In 1961, when the exclusionary rule was held to be enforceable in state cases as well as federal cases, the United States Supreme Court wrote:

There are those who say, as did Justice (then Judge) Cardozo, that, under our constitutional exclusionary doctrine, "[t]he criminal is to go free because the constable has blundered.' In some cases, this will undoubtedly be the result." Mapp v. Ohio, 367 U.S. 643 (1961).

Mapp was a landmark case and its impact on the law of criminal procedure continues to resonate today. The *Mapp* case underscores that evidence seized in violation of the United States Constitution will generally be suppressed. The primary purpose of the exclusionary rule is to deter governmental misconduct and overreaching. This focus was apparent when the Court held that:

Our decision, founded on reason and truth, gives to the individual no more than that which the Constitution guarantees him, to the police officer no less than that to which honest law enforcement is entitled, and, to the courts, that judicial integrity so necessary in the true administration of justice.

When cases fail because of a lack of probable cause, the impacts can be felt beyond the case itself. Officers can become the subjects of internal complaints, remedial or disciplinary actions, civil lawsuits, or even criminal charges. The reality of the exclusionary rule is that the bridge connecting a defendant to the evidence can quickly be shattered with significant consequences for the officers involved.

How Does Probable Cause Differ From Reasonable Suspicion?

We must note in our discussion that probable cause differs significantly from the legal concept of reasonable suspicion. These two terms are often thrown around loosely and unfortunately, there are times when they are used interchangeably. For law enforcement officers, understanding the distinction between them is critical.

Legally, reasonable suspicion requires a lesser degree of certainty of criminal activity than does probable cause. Think of it occupying a lower rung on the evidence ladder. The main difference between the standards can be seen in terms of their overall probability. If you are investigating an incident and uncover evidence, can you say that the evidence shows that criminal activity is *probable* (probable cause) or is it merely *suspected* (reasonable suspicion)? Another good question to ask yourself is "Does the evidence provide answers, or does it create more questions?"

Notably, reasonable suspicion is commonly established by a series of behaviors that are only *suspected* of being unlawful. If these behaviors were *actually* unlawful, then the higher standard of probable cause has been reached. Think about it. If you have met the probable cause threshold, *you are no longer questioning whether or not you are authorized to make an arrest or conduct a search.* This becomes the critical difference between the two standards. Remember the factors that create reasonable suspicion are oftentimes lawful when viewed in isolation but raise the specter of criminal wrongdoing when viewed in their totality. Let's take a closer look.

At the start of your shift, you attend roll call. Your sergeant advises that there have been several recent thefts from unoccupied cars in the ABC Mall's main parking lot.

Later, while you are on patrol, you drive through the lot to perform an area check. You observe someone walking quickly between parked cars. He is carrying a black duffel bag, and he seems to be systematically looking in the windows of several unoccupied vehicles. As you discreetly observe him, you note that prior to him peering into the cars, he glances around to see if anyone is watching him.

Now what? Would it be proper for you to approach him? If not, why? If so, would your approach be based on probable cause or reasonable suspicion? Let us break it down by asking the following questions:

- **Is it illegal for someone to walk between parked cars in a public parking lot?**
- **Is it illegal for someone to carry a duffel bag in a public parking lot?**
- **Is it illegal for someone to look in a car's windows in a public parking lot?**

Clearly, these actions in isolation are not unlawful. However, when they are viewed collectively alongside the earlier information you received, do they raise your suspicions? Of course, they do. Given these circumstances, it would be entirely reasonable for you to approach him and investigate. While they do not provide you with sufficient evidence to make an arrest or to search his duffel bag, they may justify a brief detention for you to confirm or dispel your reasonable suspicions. If, during that detention, you learn that the suspect was in possession of stolen property, then you would have entered the realm of probable cause and would be authorized to make an arrest. If no criminal activity was confirmed, then your brief detention would conclude without criminal charges.

Practically speaking, the distinction between the two standards can be a fine one. Knowing this, officers should be mindful of the context of the facts that they learn, since different conditions may require different responses.

A Consistent Framework

In the world of police report writing, the devil is in the details. New officers, when documenting reasonable suspicion or probable cause, should always employ a consistent framework. Doing so will help them in categorizing newly acquired information by considering its apparent relevance or importance. Facts, for the most part, usually land within one of three silos. They tend to (1) confirm (or at least suggest) a connection to a crime or event, (2) demonstrate that no connection exists, or (3) fall short of sufficient information to make a reasonable judgment one way or the other.

Our framework starts with the premise that officers must *decide* when they have learned sufficient information to act. And that decision to act must be reasonable. Put another way: there must be a *logical nexus between the information officers learn and the actions they take because of that information.* For instance, a pat-down search for weapons is lawful under certain circumstances (more on this later). Generally, there must be a reasonable belief that the person detained is potentially armed. But the officer's search for weapons, barring other factors, would not justify a strip search for narcotics. It is not that strip searches are per se illegal. Rather, strip searches just exceed the parameters of a protective pat-down.

In an evolving situation, an officer's *actions, reactions, or decisions not to act* must be logically related to the information presented. Here, the possibilities of nuance are endless, but trained law enforcement officers should possess the professional acumen to diagnose an event. They should be able to determine whether a matter is civil or criminal, whether they must restore order, whether they need to intervene, and so on.

A helpful question to ask, then, when employing this framework is "What do I currently know and what do I need to know?" Here is another example.

While on patrol, you see someone driving at 20 mph over the posted speed limit. You decide to conduct a motor vehicle stop to investigate. When you speak to the driver, you sense that she is nervous, and observe her fidgeting.

What can you do with this limited information?

- **Is there any reason to suspect that she is armed?**
- **Is there any reason to suspect that she is driving under the influence?**
- **What caused her to speed?**
- **What is causing her nervousness?**
- **Is there probable cause to search her or the vehicle?**

What if we added the fact that she was seen leaving an area where gunshots were heard and her car matched the description of the fleeing vehicle? How about if she was seen staggering out of a bar and nearly striking another vehicle as she drove off?

As you can see, with the addition of each new fact, the needle moves towards a greater probability that an offense is reasonably suspected or even probable. It is not reasonable to think that a traffic violation, on its own, provides an officer with sufficient probable cause to arrest a person for a weapons offense or for driving under the influence. A traffic violation certainly provides the officer with justification to *stop* the vehicle. But the violation could have been caused by inadvertence, a medical issue, inexperience, lack of driving skill, and so on.

As additional information is added, though, a clearer picture begins to emerge. Physical indicators, like slurred speech or bloodshot eyes, or visible evidence such as an empty box of ammunition, may offer clues that require the officer to investigate further. In this way, the traffic violation *could* be indicative of flight from a crime scene or the operator's overall fitness to drive. But there must be some sort of logical relationship established first.

If you were the investigating officer here, there would come a point when, based on the information you have, you would need to determine your next step. It may be that no further action is justified, or it could be that evidence provides reasonable suspicion for a protective pat down or probable cause for a search or arrest. It is your training, experience, and knowledge of the law that will be your guide.

Suffice it to say that, as you gain experience, your ability to identify reasonable suspicion or probable cause will improve. However, officers must possess a fundamental knowledge of these concepts from the beginning since the law requires that they act with reason and prudence. Failure to do so can be problematic. Officers must perform their duties in a way consistent with what another trained police officer would do in the same or similar circumstances.

Here is another example using a trespass investigation:

- **Officer Adams is on patrol and observes two young males walking out of a private wooded area. There is no posted sign, but the area is surrounded by a split rail fence. Officer Adams decides to stop and investigate.**

Now consider these questions:

- **Are Officer Adams' actions based on reasonable suspicion or probable cause?**
- **Would there be a difference if Officer Adams had been requested by the property owner?**
- **How might Officer Adams be able to confirm whether the young males were trespassing?**

These, and other questions, are important here. Even though trespassing is a relatively minor criminal offense, it provides a good example of the reasoned analysis that must occur during an investigation. When facts or circumstances change, officers might have to modify their response.

In this example, a reasonable and prudent police officer would be aware that trespassing is a criminal offense. Trespassers must be given *prior notice* that they are prohibited from entering onto the property of another. If trespassers fail to heed this warning, there is a presumption that they intend to trespass. This means that trespassing generally occurs when trespassers enter someone's land after being previously asked to leave, or when they pass a physical barrier that gives notice that entry is not permitted, such as a posted sign.

On the other hand, if permission is given by the property owner, no crime has occurred. An invite negates a critical element in the crime of trespassing.

With this background, let's consider the scenario again. If Officer Adams was on patrol and observed the young males on the property, her detention of them would be based on *reasonable suspicion only*. Additional information would be needed to confirm whether a crime had occurred. Consequently, it would be improper for Officer Adams to make an arrest because, at this point, she can only reasonably suspect criminal activity.

However, if the property owner had called the police because trespassers were seen on the property, and the owner confirmed that they did not have authority to enter, the needle moves towards criminality. Officer Adams would learn that the young males' presence on the property was not permitted. Remember, though, that Officer Adams would need to confirm that they had been (1) previously told that they could not enter the property or (2) had disregarded a posted sign or other physical barrier. If so, probable cause would be established to make an arrest since, based on the totality of these circumstances, the crime of trespassing would be *probable.*

Experienced officers recognize that establishing probable cause can be a fluid exercise. There are times when probable cause is obvious, such as when a person is observed intentionally striking another. However, the opposite also exists, and evidence must be uncovered. Consider the following scenario:

Officer Adams responds to a bar fight at a local tavern. When she arrives, she observes Joe and Jennifer being separated by several bystanders. Joe has swelling to his right hand, and Jennifer has blood dripping from her nose.

As part of her responsibilities, Officer Adams must determine:

- **The identities of the people involved.**
- **The nature of the relationship between Joe and Jennifer, such as whether they are strangers or if they have a domestic relationship.**
- **The cause of the physical fight.**
- **Whether there was provocation or mitigating factors present.**
- **A determination of who was the aggressor.**

And the list goes on. To make these determinations, Officer Adams has several available options. She can speak with witnesses. She can check for surveillance cameras. She can interview Joe and Jennifer.

If, for instance, Officer Adams determines that Joe and Jennifer are romantically involved, she will need to conduct a domestic violence investigation. Domestic violence statutes typically mandate arrests when probable cause establishes that a crime has occurred.

For purposes of this example, imagine that Joe and Jennifer are engaged. They went out for the evening and became involved in a verbal argument over their finances. Two separate eyewitnesses stated that they heard Joe say, "One more comment and I'll pop you." Shortly thereafter, Joe struck Jennifer in the face with his right fist, and the two witnesses intervened. A third person also witnessed the strike and called the police.

Based on these facts, there is sufficient probable cause for Officer Adams to arrest Joe for domestic assault and battery. Officer Adams established that Joe and Jennifer were in a "domestic" relationship; three "independent" witnesses gave corroborating statements that Joe threatened to strike Jennifer, and then did so; Jennifer sustained a visible injury from the strike; and Joe sustained visible injury to his hand. With this evidence, a reasonable and prudent police officer investigating the incident could reach the logical conclusion that Joe, more likely than not, intentionally struck Jennifer with his fist.

The fluidity of probable cause will change as circumstances do. This investigation would assuredly be different if there were no witnesses, or the witnesses provided contradictory accounts. Good investigators will ask probing questions to uncover information and will seek available resources as they progress through their investigations. They will identify vital details, uncover inconsistencies, and determine what actions are most appropriate. Subtle details can profoundly impact a case and it is up to investigators to identify them. And these details must find their way into the report narrative:

Reasonable Suspicion and Documenting a Protective Pat-Down

Any discussion of search and seizure law, probable cause, or reasonable suspicion would not be complete without a review of the law involving pat-down searches. Commonly, these limited searches yield evidence, even though their main function is safety. In this area of criminal procedure, the most important case for officers to understand is *Terry v. Ohio. Terry* set the national standard for an officer's authority to conduct a limited search for weapons. It differentiated between searches having a primary purpose of locating evidence of a crime and those seeking to protect the investigating officer from harm.

In certain circumstances, when officers develop reasonable suspicion to stop and briefly detain a person, they may conduct a limited pat-down search for weapons. A pat-down search is deemed lawful when the officer reasonably believes that the person detained may be armed. The Supreme Court in *Terry* held that:

Our evaluation of the proper balance that has to be struck in this type of case leads us to conclude that there must be a narrowly drawn authority to permit a reasonable search for weapons for the protection of the police officer, where he has reason to believe that he is dealing with an armed and dangerous individual, regardless of whether he has probable cause to arrest the individual for a crime. The officer need not be absolutely certain that the individual is armed; the issue is whether a reasonably prudent man, in the circumstances, would be warranted in the belief that his safety or that of others was in danger. And in determining whether the officer acted reasonably in such circumstances, due weight must be given not to his inchoate and unparticularized suspicion or "hunch," but to the specific reasonable inferences which he is entitled to draw from the facts in light of his experience. Terry v. Ohio, 392 U.S. 1, 30 27 (1968) (internal citations omitted).

A police report detailing a limited pat-down search for weapons requires that officers clearly articulate the basis of their reasonable suspicion. In the *Terry* case, the officer explained that his extensive law enforcement experience led him to suspect that several men were casing a store. He noted that his suspicion was aroused by "their measured pacing, peering, and conferring" which was described as "elaborately casual and oft-repeated reconnaissance of the store window" and the officer indicated that he suspected a "casing a job, a stick-up" and approached them.

The details the officer articulated in the *Terry* case were sufficient to demonstrate that his pat-down search was reasonable. As a result, the gun located during the search was deemed admissible as evidence and led to the defendant's conviction.

Officers will be greatly assisted by understanding common legal standards, especially when it comes to writing their narratives. This does not mean that officers must define legal standards in their reports. Rather, they should be aware of the standards that apply to policing and then describe how their actions conformed to those standards. It usually comes down to the difference between labeling behavior and describing behavior. Officers must recognize that information needs to be explained beyond "*I conducted a pat-down search for my safety.*" For instance:

When I approached Jones, I saw him quickly place his right hand in his jacket pocket. He was perspiring and kept glancing at my firearm. When I asked Jones to remove his hand from his pocket, he refused. Fearing for my safety, I conducted a pat-down search for weapons. During the search, I located a switchblade in the right front pocket of his jacket.

In this example, you, as the investigating officer, are describing Jones' behavior rather than just labeling it. Your perspective of the event is critical, and the report is your opportunity to explain why your limited pat-down search for weapons was justified. Any later judicial review of your decision will not include the benefit of hindsight since your perceptions at the time of the event are the primary focus.

The Importance of
How Facts Are Learned

Witnesses represent one of the primary sources of information for police officers. Although there are instances when officers learn information first-hand – such as when they personally observe someone commit a crime – much of what officers uncover comes from second or third-hand information. In many cases, the reporting parties themselves may not have been direct witnesses.

In every instance, it is vital that officers report information exactly as it was relayed. If officers describe second or third-hand information as if they had personally observed it, they then adopt the others' accounts as unequivocal facts. And witness accounts, of course, may not be accurate.

Officers who fall into this trap typically do so unintentionally. They may fail to use informational qualifiers in their report, such as "the witness reported" or "the witness alleged," instead describing events as if they had observed them firsthand. This is a mistake that can have a significant impact on an investigation.

Let us consider this using our previous example of Officer Adams, who responded to a physical fight between Joe and Jennifer. Since Officer Adams did not personally witness the incident, she needed to utilize other avenues of investigation. This, of course, included obtaining witness statements and making visual observations of the scene and the people involved. Knowing this, which of the following statements would be recommended when Officer Adams writes her report?

While he was seated inside the bar, Joe Jones struck Jennifer Jones in the face.

OR

One of the witnesses, later identified as John Smith, told me that he witnessed the fight between Joe Jones and Jennifer Jones. Smith stated that he observed Joe Jones strike Jennifer Jones in the face.

You can see that in the second example, Officer Adams goes further in describing the information that she learned. While Officer Adams' first statement gives the appearance that she personally witnessed the fight, or at least knows it to be true, her second statement more accurately qualifies the information by showing how she learned it. As the case progresses, Officer Adams may identify additional information that either corroborates or refutes Smith's account. This is the very essence of conducting a complete investigation.

As first responders, officers are routinely dispatched to events that have occurred in the past. This means that they must piece together the facts.

The determinations they make can have significant impacts, such as when an officer makes an arrest or performs a search that yields incriminating evidence. In all instances, it is essential for officers to recognize that *facts learned are just that – facts learned.* In their narratives, it is imperative that officers describe not just the information, but *how* they obtained that information.

Moving on with the previous example, imagine that Officer Adams was able to make observations that were consistent with what she learned from the witness.

Upon my arrival, I observed that Joe Jones and Jennifer Jones were being separated by two bystanders. The bystanders were later identified as Richard Ross and Pete Johnson. Initially, I observed that Jennifer Jones had blood dripping from her nose, and she was yelling "Please get him away from me." I also observed that Joe Jones had visible redness and swelling to his right hand.

Although Officer Adams had not directly witnessed the altercation, the observations she made were consistent with the others' accounts of the fight. This is the heart of an investigation.

Each relevant fact or inference that an officer learns should work to either prove or disprove an aspect of the case. In this way, facts and inferences become the evidentiary compass used by an officer to identify an investigative path, while the report narrative becomes the instrument to show why that path was reasonable.

Summary

The difference between criminal and noncriminal investigations can sometimes be elusive. Officers must become adept at navigating through the many nuances of circumstance, since small factual changes can greatly influence which road a case travels. Regardless of the nature of a case, though, an articulate, balanced, and comprehensive report is essential.

When cases become criminal investigations, a person's liberty interests are at stake. This means that many constitutional safeguards and rules of procedure are triggered. In law enforcement, officers must have a thorough understanding of the legal thresholds required for official action, such as probable cause and reasonable suspicion. At the same time, they must recognize the pitfalls and potential impacts of reaching beyond those thresholds. Nowhere is this more apparent than in the application of the exclusionary rule.

Chapter 4
Police Reports Cannot
Be a Road to Nowhere!

Police reports must be understandable. Unfortunately, there are some who view report writing as an inconvenience or afterthought. Reports may be rushed or even ignored altogether. There are many dangers to taking this approach.

The process of documenting a crime or event is not an exercise in futility. In the criminal justice system, a poorly written police report can result in an unjust case outcome. Beyond that, unsatisfactory police reports reflect poorly on the officers writing them, on their agency, and on the law enforcement profession as a whole.

In truth, the report writing process is challenging and time consuming. This is especially true when new officers are tasked with a complex case. Making the adjustment from observer to investigator is difficult, but then moving from investigator to illustrator takes practice. The ability to convert one's observations and actions into a logical, coherent narrative takes on added importance when the report describes the taking of a person's liberty. This is the case when officers must make an arrest, use force, or otherwise detain a person. In this way, officers who are beginning their careers should start by reading as many police reports as they can, especially those written by more experienced officers.

Reports Must Speak to the Reader in Understandable Ways

The general police report should not contain acronyms, police jargon, slang terms, humor, or sarcasm. They are official documents written for a vital purpose and should omit inappropriate commentary. Likewise, police reports cannot demonstrate partiality or express animus towards a person or group. And, importantly, an officer's use of unclear terminology should always be avoided. Consider the following statement:

- **At the end of the incident, John Jones was given PR.**

What does this statement mean? Was Jones given public recognition? Was he released on personal recognizance? Did he receive travel tickets to Puerto Rico? In this case, PR represents the terms of Jones' release on "personal recognizance," but it is an acronym that can open to more than one reasonable interpretation and should be avoided.

How about this statement?

- **On April 1, 2022, at approximately 1200 hours, I, Officer Adams, responded to a 1200 complaint at 98 OBD.**

While the above statement may make sense to the members of Officer Adams' police agency, it does not to the layperson reading the report. The use of police jargon – here, the code "1200" – creates a circumstance where the reader is not provided with adequate information. Police report narratives require plain, unambiguous language. Revised, the above statement would read as follows:

- **On April 1, 2022, at approximately 1200 hours, I, Officer Adams, responded to a larceny complaint at 98 Ocean Bay Drive.**

Acronyms are helpful for brevity and provide a means of shorthand, but they can also lead to confusion. Here are examples of some common acronyms that officers will likely see in their career:

- **APB – "All Points Bulletin"**
- **BAC – "Blood Alcohol Content"**
- **B and E – "Breaking and Entering"**
- **BOLO – "Be on the Lookout"**
- **CAD – "Computer Aided Dispatch"**
- **ETA – "Estimated Time of Arrival"**
- **EtOH – "Alcohol"**
- **FTA – "Failure to Appear"**
- **ICS – "Incident Command System"**
- **MO – "Modus Operandi"**

- **MVA – "Motor Vehicle Accident"**
- **OD – "Overdose"**
- **PC – "Probable Cause" or "Protective Custody"**

Since we know that police officers must impartially enforce the law, it naturally follows that they must use good judgment and common sense when they write their reports. Any statements that are slanted, sprinkled with sarcasm, or that use slang terms without context, serve no legitimate purpose in a police report. In fact, statements like these can paint officers in an unfavorable light and may undermine the credibility of an investigation. This is an avoidable problem. But what does it look like?

Suppose that Officer Adams is dispatched to search for a motorcycle suspected of drag racing. As he canvasses the area, he locates the motorcycle in the parking lot of a nearby convenience store. Which of the following statements would be better suited for the officer's police report?

- **I located the bike in the lot of ABC Convenience Store. It was, of course, a crotch-rocket with a loud exhaust.**

OR

- **I located the suspected motorcycle in the parking lot of ABC Convenience Store. It was a Honda, sport type motorcycle, bearing Massachusetts registration 12345. The motorcycle's exhaust system had been modified and produced excessive noise.**

You can see that the second example provides more details while lacking the sarcasm or slang terminology of the first example. The reader may perceive from the first statement that Officer Adams has a negative predisposition towards racing style motorcycles. While this may not be the case, Officer Adams' word choice inevitably leaves that impression on the reader.

This is not to say that slang terms, offensive statements, or vulgar language are entirely prohibited from police reports. At times, their use in a police report is appropriate when the context provides for it, such as when a suspect's direct quote is relevant to a case or when statements give an officer investigative direction. Here are a few examples:

- **As I approached the suspect, I observed that he was clenching his fists and staring at my firearm. The suspect then yelled, "Screw you, pig" at me several times.**
- **I spoke to William James, who told me that he witnessed the shooting. James described the suspect as a white male with a black baseball cap, who was carrying what he described as a "black burner" in his right hand. The term "burner" is a commonly used slang reference to a handgun or firearm.**

The use of quotations distinctly tells the reader that the statement came from someone besides the officer. Similarly, the use of direct quotations can be powerful evidence, especially when they are indicative of a person's state of mind. Typical examples of this would include when a suspect makes a spontaneous utterance or when a victim statement demonstrates a present sense impression. In a report narrative, the reader should know when the officer has switched gears. Credibility is essential in policing, and anything less can lead to erosion of a community's trust. This, in turn, can render the police agency ineffective.

What's the "Story" With the Report?

The purpose of a police report is to provide information to the reader. It transmits information for the many purposes that we have already discussed – and more. But while a report will tell a story, it must *not* exaggerate any details or be, in any way, a fictional account.

We know that traditional storytelling provides entertainment value. This is not to say that fictional storytelling or symbolic historical stories cannot inform a reader or provide an educational message. Some of our most important cultural lessons have been passed down through generations through storytelling. Countless people have learned important life lessons through age-old fables or parables. Even the entertainment industry knows that real life stories can be interesting – and profitable. However, there is no place in a police report for facts to be dramatized or injected with hyperbole.

The "story" provided in a police report is unique. There is no "audience" in the entertainment sense, although law enforcement cases have supplied ingredients for numerous television shows, movies, and books. Instead, the report simply tells the reader what occurred and what law enforcement did as a result.

Sadly, some of the calls that officers handle defy logic and demonstrate the worst of humanity. In fact, during my career, I cannot tell you how many times I have heard another officer say, "You can't make this s*** up!" when describing a case. *But case facts are what they are.* As challenging as some investigations can be, officers must take their cases as they find them, and then do their best to carry out their professional duties. In every sense of the word, the investigative story must always be one of objectivity.

We all know from our school days that a story contains several distinct parts. Typically, there is an introduction, a plot, a setting, and a conclusion. Traditional stories contain tension and conflict while exploring relationships. Some stories are open-ended and leave the reader speculating about possible outcomes. Some are conveniently closed and happily resolved. All combine to create a lure while simultaneously triggering the reader's imagination.

In the case of a police narrative, the totality of the investigative story should provide the reader with a clear picture of *precisely what happened.* Any void in the "story" should be pointed out for what it is – an unknown – since a police report should not leave a reader guessing. When specific information is undetermined, an officer must inform the reader of that fact. Here are some examples of officers referencing information that is not yet known:

- **I conducted a canvass of the area, but I was unable to identify any witnesses to the theft.**
- **When I arrived on scene, I observed that there was some visible red paint transfer to the right rear bumper of Smith's vehicle. This suggested that the suspect's vehicle was red in color, but the type of vehicle has not yet been determined.**

Along with accurately answering questions, a police report should also be contextually clear. In this way, the background information provided by the officer allows the reader to stand in the officer's shoes. After spending many years writing and reading police reports, I know that good narratives not only tell the reader about the officer's actions and observations, but also *why it was necessary* for the officer to be present in the first place. As you might imagine, there are countless reasons that can prompt police-citizen contacts.

Did someone request police? Did the officer conduct a traffic stop? Did another agency ask for help?

The nuanced reasons prompting a call for service often dictate how an officer approaches the scene. For instance, if a caller tells a dispatcher that an armed person is creating a disturbance, that information becomes vital for the safety of the responding officer and others. In that case, the officer may opt for a clandestine approach. Likewise, a call may suggest that the officer will face exigent circumstances, such as when dispatched to a bomb threat or active assailant situation. Remember that officers are bound by procedural, statutory, and policy driven duties, so the reasons for an officer's actions are usually guided by the circumstances. Consider these questions as we move on in this chapter:

- **Do you think that the speed of an officer's response should differ depending on the type of call?**
- **If so, what types of factors do you think are important to consider?**
- **When do you think that lights and sirens are appropriate? When are they not?**
- **How might an officer's response to a burglary in progress differ from a response to vandalism that occurred three hours prior?**
- **What would happen if the officer was involved in a crash on the way to a call?**

These questions are representative of the complexity of present-day law enforcement. Officers must be trained. Their actions must be reasonable. They must be adaptable and capable of thinking on their feet. While your agency's policy for answering calls will dictate the types of situations that require a priority response, your common sense, training, and experience will also give you guidance. The purposes of these questions are not to make you commit to an answer, but rather to get you in the habit of asking them. This way, you can preemptively evaluate the circumstances you may face, and modify your actions as needed. This provides you with the best opportunity for identifying proper solutions.

Legally, law enforcement decisions will be evaluated in terms of reasonableness. No event in the police field creates more administrative and legal review than a use of force, a topic covered in detail in Chapter 8. The Supreme Court in *Graham v. Connor* specifically noted that in use of force cases, the totality of the circumstances facing an officer must be considered without the benefit of hindsight or deliberation. This means that any reviewer must be aware of the officer's predicament, since officers "are often forced to make split-second judgments – in circumstances that are tense, uncertain, and rapidly evolving[.]" In order for the reader to fully appreciate what the officer faced, the events must be adequately described.

For instance, officers who are quickly confronted by a combative person may not have the luxury of time to contemplate how to respond. They may be required to immediately take control of the person by force to protect themselves or others from harm. Similarly, an officer who places a suicidal person in handcuffs for that person's protection, and not for a criminal offense, must demonstrate that such action was appropriate. How this is articulated in a report becomes critically important.

Beyond use of force situations, officers will encounter calls where they take other forms of official action. Their actions may be procedurally or statutorily permissible, or they may be recommended as a best practice. A good example of this is the plain view doctrine. Under this legal principle, officers are generally authorized to seize any unlawful items that they observe. This could be an illegally possessed controlled substance, an unlicensed firearm, or a piece of stolen property. However, to do so, they must first be lawfully present in the location where the item is observed, whether public or private. Here are some examples:

- **Officers observed a person selling suspected drugs in a public park. The transaction took place out in the open. They determined the suspected drugs were heroin and arrested the drug purchaser and the drug buyer. They also seized the money transacted and the cache of illegal drugs.**
- **Officers responded to a private home for a noise complaint and were invited inside. When they entered the house, they observed a gun on the kitchen table. As a result, they arrested the occupant for improper storage of a firearm and seized the weapon.**
- **An officer conducted a traffic stop for speeding. Clearly visible on the front passenger seat was an opened box of illegal fireworks.**

The officer seized the box and its contents and arrested the driver for unlawful possession of fireworks.

The key here is lawful presence, but the underlying lesson is that officers must have a solid grasp of their authority as well as its limits. Importantly, as we previously discussed, there are prohibitions against the government's overreach, and when violations are found, courts can take corrective action. One of the most impactful of these measures is when evidence of a crime is suppressed by operation of the exclusionary rule as discussed in Chapter 3.

In a police narrative, the underlying circumstances of a case must provide the reader with context for the official actions that follow. This is critical, especially when those actions are later challenged in court. It begins with officers being aware of the important investigative questions that help establish the framework for the narrative. These questions, along with officers' use of their five senses, give them the necessary tools to formulate a detailed picture. It helps to demonstrate to the reader (1) what they saw and what they did, (2) why they did so, (3) how they resolved or attempted to resolve a situation, and (4) whether a follow-up investigation was required or recommended. In this way, the common police report acts as an investigative roadmap.

Before we discuss basic narrative writing, we will briefly touch upon the differences between the structure and substance of a police report and why these differences are so significant.

Structure

The structure of a police report narrative refers to how it is organized. It consists of the overall arrangement of the information conveyed. While answers to those important questions of "who, what, where, when, why, and how?" remain substance-based inquiries that will be discussed below, the order in which those questions are asked make up the structure of the police report. To be effective, narratives must be organized, coherent, and chronological.

This is by design. The person reading a police report must be able to visualize the events as they occurred, with each piece of information leading logically to the next. Since the reasonableness of an officer's actions is commonly a focal point of review, the report should generally describe the events the officer faced *as they happened.*

Think about this as being analogous to the construction of a new house. Before the roof is installed, the house needs to have walls. Before the walls, it needs a foundation. It is simply a matter of sequence. In many ways, policing is no different. The facts officers learn and the evidence they uncover frequently establishes the next steps in their investigative routes.

For example, an officer who discovers a bloodstain on a doorknob must first inspect that bloodstain. Does it contain fingerprint ridge detail? Is it a transfer stain or spatter? What is the underlying crime being investigated? Depending on the circumstances, there may be different investigative paths required. If the case is minor, the officer may only need to take photographs. If the case involves a serious crime, the bloodstain may require collection and preservation for DNA analysis. If the officer is not certified in processing trace evidence, a trained crime scene technician may be summoned. You get the picture.

In addition, a police report should not fluctuate between topics or time frames without the officer making logical connections. At a minimum, an incoherent structure can lead to confusion by the reader. The greater the confusion, the greater the chance for a case dismissal or unsuccessful prosecution.

Consider, for a moment, an arrest report. Those taken into custody for a criminal offense forfeit their personal liberty, either temporarily or permanently. If a case eventually fails because the arresting officer did not properly document the progression of the investigation, the fallout can be disastrous.

What follows is a graphic organizer that can be used to assist you in organizing your reports. Even though police reports are not "one size fits all", this tool offers a helpful starting point and some general factors to consider.

You can see that each box represents a different report paragraph. The various boxes include common operational considerations, as well as a checklist for some of the duties that an officer may wish to remember. Likewise, it offers guidance for prioritizing policing responsibilities, such as when an officer is required to act before the "investigative process" begins. A good example of this is when a police officer must direct traffic at a crash scene before they can take witness statements or determine the causal factors of the crash. The report narrative that you write may deviate from what is provided here. Remember that this is not a mandatory format for police reports but rather a general guide.

*general guidelines for common police reports where you are dispatched to a call and person(s) are on scene when you arrive.

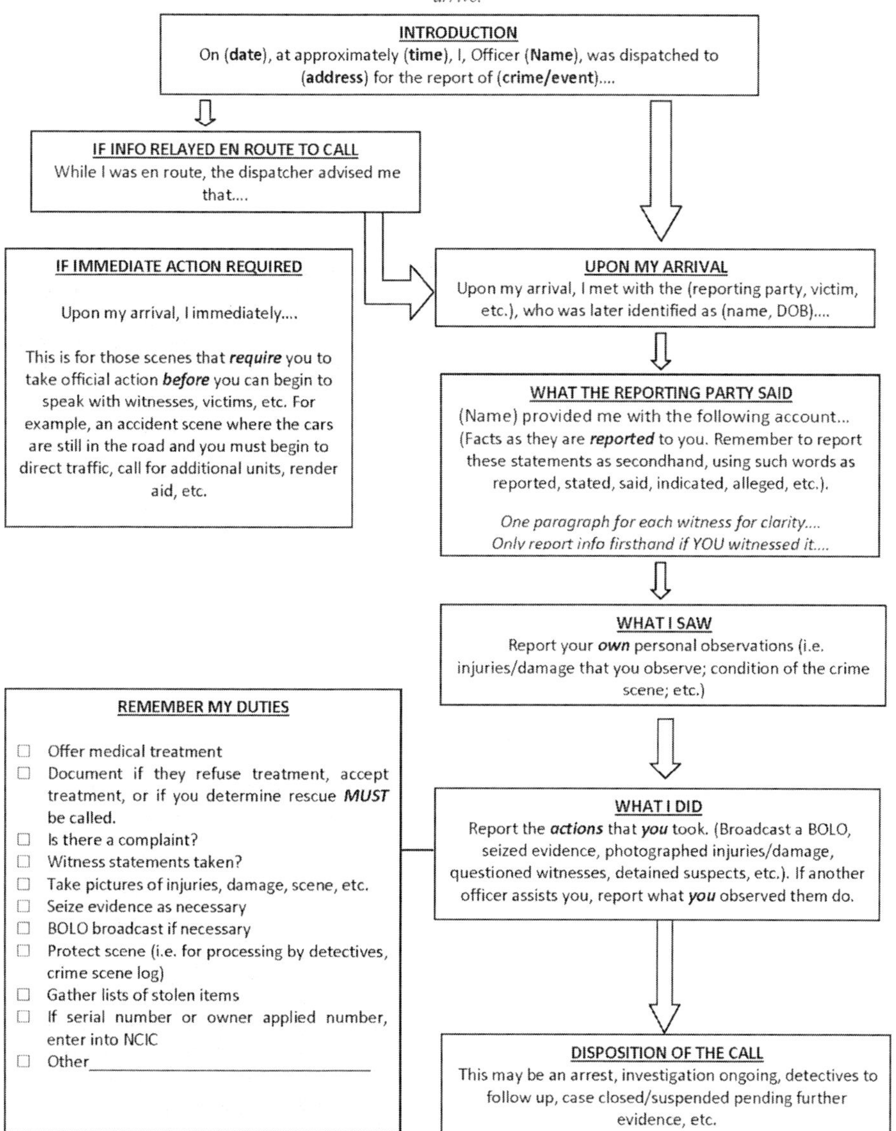

Substance

Substance is the information that is incorporated into a report's framework. Whereas structure shapes a police report, substance fills it in. Using the human body as an analogy, structure would be a person's skeleton, while substance would be the flesh and organs.

When we consider the importance of substance in a police report, it makes sense to start with the premise that the responding officer was (1) in a specific place, (2) at a specific time, (3) for a specific reason. This will help in answering the all-important investigative questions of "who, what, where, when, why, and how". Consider the following example of an introductory statement in a police report:

On June 12, 2020, at approximately 1000 hours, I, Officer Adams, was dispatched to 956 Elm Street for the report of a vandalized motor vehicle.

In just one sentence, several questions have been answered.

- *Who* **responded? Officer Adams.**
- *Where* **did Officer Adams respond? 956 Elm Street.**
- *When* **did Officer Adams respond? On June 12, 2020, at 1000 hours.**
- *Why* **did Officer Adams respond? To investigate the report of a vandalized motor vehicle.**

Granted, the complexity of the investigation could conceivably require multiple answers to each of the questions. The question of "who?" might refer to responding officers, victims, suspects, witnesses, reporting parties, and so on. However, keeping each of these questions at the forefront of your mind will allow you to hone your investigative focus. Recognizing not only the need for information, but also why it is needed, will improve your skills as a trained observer.

Substance also makes up the subject matter of a case. In a crime report, an example of substance would be how the officer established and then documented the elements of a crime. While we will discuss these legal requirements in greater detail in Chapter 5, it bears mentioning that each crime element represents a distinctive box that must be checked before an officer can charge a person with a criminal offense. But what does that mean?

Consider, for example, the crime of larceny (theft). This offense is generally defined as the taking of another's property with the intent to permanently deprive the rightful owner of that property. In the legal sense, this means that a suspect intends to *take title* to the property, which is just another way of saying the "taking" is *for good.* As a result, the police narrative for a larceny investigation must contain facts that demonstrate that the suspect was not merely *borrowing or holding* the item. Rather, the investigating officer must show that, in addition to just taking the item, the suspect *intended to steal* it. This can be demonstrated by actions, such as the suspect attempting to sell the property, or altering the item in some way. If the facts do not demonstrate the suspect's intention to steal, then the crime of larceny cannot be established. It's as simple as that.

This, however, is not to say that without evidence of the suspect's intention to steal, no crime occurred or that another criminal charge is unwarranted. Rather, the facts may just demonstrate that the elements of a different crime were met, such as the suspect unlawfully possessing another's property. In every case, the most reliable guide is evidence.

When a police report contains sufficient substance, it does not leave the reader speculating about why an officer took certain actions. Instead, the reader should be able to reach the conclusion that the officer acted reasonably given the circumstances. For instance, if you were reading a police report about a car stop, the officer's narrative may note the excess speed the vehicle was traveling and the tool the officer used to confirm that speed (i.e., radar). The officer may explain how the vehicle changed lanes without signaling a turn or ran a red light, and so on.

Correspondingly, good police reports explain why certain information was missing from the report. It sounds strange to say that officers should describe information that is missing or unknown, but this is exceptionally important in keeping an investigation in proper context. Consider the following police report excerpt discussing a witness's observations during a robbery. In this instance, even though the witness saw the robbery suspect, she was unable to provide any specific details about his facial features.

Jones told me she witnessed the entire robbery. She said that the male suspect was approximately six feet in height and was wearing a black and white ski mask. Jones reported that the mask covered most of the suspect's face, except for his jawline, which she described as unshaven with black and gray beard growth. She said that due to the mask, she was unable to see any other features of the suspect's face.

As investigators, law enforcement officers must always strive for thoroughness. This is one of the most effective ways to provide readers with insight into each of the conditions the officer faced.

Report Objectivity – A Balancing Act?

How do you think a case would fare if a report demonstrated a police officer's personal dislike for a suspect? How about his or her dislike of a group of people? Would it matter if the officer had no personal animus towards the person or group, but submitted a narrative that was written poorly and gave that impression?

This is not a rhetorical question. We must consider the real-world implications of poorly written reports. The corollary to the statement *"if it's not in the report, it didn't happen"* is the statement *"if it's in the report, it did happen."* The subject matter of a report can always be challenged by those impacted by it, and typically, challenges come in the form of arguments advanced by a defense attorney. Reasonable implications from reports are quite impactful, whether or not those implications reflect poorly on the issuing officer.

Objectivity is the cornerstone of a high-quality police investigation. Beginning on day one of the training academy, law enforcement recruits will continuously be reminded of the importance of integrity and impartiality. There can be no alternative. It is very telling that law enforcement members work in the criminal *justice* system, not the criminal *conviction* system. In a nutshell, this means that truthfulness remains the fundamental component of a criminal investigation. Officers are duty-bound to report both inculpatory and exculpatory information that is learned during an investigation. Only then, can one of the primary goals of the law enforcement profession be attained – that justice is served.

As you might imagine, an active crime scene can be tumultuous. It will require that officers think on their feet and revert to their training. Crime scenes can also be unsettling and touch on politically sensitive areas. The impact of an officer's word choices in describing a scene can become the subject of controversy, especially if the words used can be easily misconstrued.

This creates an unmistakable tension. On one hand, poor word choice can be inflammatory. On the other, the officer has a duty to accurately document information. In essence, although officers must remain mindful of incendiary language and delicate subjects, there is no requirement that they sanitize the circumstances they encounter.

What Did You Say?

Let us imagine that a police officer interviews a Native American witness at a crash scene. Later, that Native American is described as an "Indian" in the officer's report narrative. What is your first impression of the officer? Does this officer sound objective or biased to you? Does it matter if the officer's use of the term is unconnected to the causal factors of the car accident itself? Does this undermine the credibility of the report?

Today, the word "Indian" is an outdated and offensive term when used to describe the Native American population. If the officer had simply been unaware of this linguistic shift, would the language choice become more defensible in your eyes? The purpose of this example is to show that errors of this nature, even when made unknowingly, can raise partiality or credibility concerns.

In a professional sense, many might find the officer's lack of familiarity with certain offensive language explainable, but still inexcusable. While police officers are humans, they carry the heavy responsibility of performing their duties impartially. If officers use offensive terms in their reports, rightly or wrongly, they may be viewed negatively by the reader. In this example, the reader may see the officer as uninformed, unintelligent, or even worse, racist. And, as a result, the officer's reputation may suffer. Worse still, if the offensive statement was made knowingly by the officer, there are likely greater concerns beyond report writing.

This can be contrasted with those times when officers will be called upon to document *others'* use of obscenities, slang terms, or informal language. Present sense impressions and spontaneous statements are vitally important pieces of evidence, especially when they illustrate a person's state of mind. For instance, a suspect who slams his fist on a table and screams, "Next time I will break your legs!" has exhibited behaviors that suggest aggressiveness or poor self-control. This may corroborate evidence pointing to the suspect as the primary aggressor in a fight and belongs in the report.

Other times, the statements themselves may be the catalyst for a criminal charge, such as when a suspect makes a verbal threat against a public official or makes a statement that meets the criteria for a hate crime. Notably, obscenities, slang terms, or informal language can serve an important evidentiary purpose in a police report.

In order to engender the view that officers are fair and impartial when a report contains this type of language, they must make logical connections between the reported statements and the investigation. Think of the subtle distinction here. The connections can provide the reader with needed context but will also show the statement's relevancy. Obscenities, slang terms, or informal language, if used by officers to describe their *own* views, can be regarded as subjective fodder more fitting for an editorial column. When those same officers describe the words of others, the importance of the statements will be instantly recognizable for their evidentiary value.

Consider this:

- **Jones was acting crazy.**

OR

- **Smith told me that Jones was "acting crazy." She stated that although there was snow and ice on the ground, Jones was barefoot as he paced in his driveway and yelled at passing cars.**

From their daily experiences, members of the law enforcement profession know all too well that the real world exists, and its underbelly is often on full display. It is the exception rather than the rule that a person calls a police dispatch center to give good news. Instead, calls for assistance are regularly made by people in crisis, in fear, or who have been victimized in some way. By investigating criminal conduct, officers regularly uncover examples of hatred, disrespect, or a general disregard for fellow human beings. When they are describing these events in their narratives, officers must always remain impartial. An officer might not have personal admiration for someone who just abused a child or exploited an elderly person, but *the officer's role is objective law enforcement, not commentary*. Training and experience will teach officers that "good" people can do bad things, and "bad" people can do good things.

Aside from their negative impacts on a criminal case, subjective police reports – whether perceived or real – just look unprofessional. The need to avoid subjectivity in the justice system is not unique to the policing world.

Any partiality in the law can easily undermine the integrity of the system as a whole. How well received would a court case be if the judge interlaced a decision with personal feelings or biased statements? What if a state social worker removed a child from a home based on their personal dislike of the child's parents? How might these types of situations impact society's faith in our governmental systems?

In practice, one of the most effective ways to avoid subjective language, even when subjectivity is unintentional, is for officers to consider the emotional effect of the words or phrases being used. The English language can be tricky. Words often have closely related synonyms, so it is important that officers, when describing events from their own point of view, use words that are less likely to be emotionally charged.

Let's say that Officer Adams is dispatched to a family disturbance. When she arrives on scene, Officer Adams locates Jane Jones, who is visibly upset. Later, when Officer Adams completes her police report, she must objectively describe Jones' demeanor in her narrative. Which of the below statements would be a more acceptable statement for Officer Adams' police report?

- **Upon my arrival, I observed that Jane Jones was sniveling.**

OR

- **Upon my arrival, I observed that Jane Jones was crying. She was tearful and had visible redness to her eyes and cheeks.**

Clearly, the second statement presents a more objective account. There is no negative tone or subjectivity, and the word choice gives the reader a more definitive view of Jones' demeanor. The word "tearful" does not engender the impassioned impression that "sniveling" does.

Another way for officers to avoid subjectivity in their police reports is to refrain from voicing their personal feelings or opinions. Editorializing is inappropriate for a police report. If judgmental language is included, an officer's personal leanings will be discernible in both subtle and non-subtle ways. This can only serve to undermine the public's trust and damage the officer's credibility. Here is an example:

- **Not being the brightest bulb, the suspect bolted east towards the ABC Gas Station, where he all but posed for a surveillance video.**

OR

- **I determined that when he heard the siren, the suspect fled the scene on foot. He reportedly ran easterly on Main Street towards the ABC Gas Station. Later, I was able to retrieve surveillance video that captured his movements.**

Again, the first statement is subjective, and it reveals the officer's not-so-subtle view of the suspect. The second statement, on the other hand, tends to provide a more dispassionate account. As a result, it is objective and more succinct.

In a narrative, statements made with hyperbole or those containing nonfactual information will undoubtedly inject error into a police report. Any lack of objectivity, however trivial, can give support to later allegations of impropriety or unprofessionalism on the part of the officer. This may result in a shift from an examination of the case to scrutiny of the investigator.

Since appropriately used crude or informal language has evidentiary value, our discussion here is to stress the importance of being aware of your language choices and remembering to *attribute words or phrases to the person who uttered them.* This is most easily accomplished by using direct quotations or paraphrased descriptions. When others' statements are reported with objectivity and clarity, the stage is set for a well-written narrative.

Spontaneous Statements

In evidence law, spontaneous statements (utterances) and present sense impressions are generally admissible at trial since they are recognized exceptions to the hearsay rule. They often provide fertile ground for uncovering evidence or a suspect's modus operandi. On impulse, a suspect may blurt out their true intentions or confirm their involvement in a crime.

In addition to their evidentiary value, these types of statements can assist in other aspects of an investigation. In law enforcement, it is not altogether uncommon for crime victims, witnesses, or others who speak to police to later recant their statements or change their accounts altogether. Their motivations for doing so can run the gamut, such as when a witness no longer wishes to be involved in a court case or when a victim fears the person arrested. Statements made *at or near the time of a crisis or event* are viewed, in the eyes of the law, as more reliable since they lack deliberation. Consequently, these will often influence investigative decisions and *must* be memorialized in the officer's narrative.

Consider the following example. If a crime victim frantically calls 911 to report an assault and battery, any statements that the person makes during the phone call will directly impact the initial stages of the case. Consider these questions:

- **What is the victim's demeanor?**
- **Are there any weapons involved?**
- **Is the incident still in progress?**
- **Has the victim described any of the suspect's actions?**

Let's say that when officers arrived, they determine that a domestic assault and battery took place and A is arrested. B is distraught and tells one of the officers that she was intentionally scratched by A. Her statement was corroborated by several visible scratches. Two days later, after reconciling with A, B seeks to recant her earlier statement to police. She tells the investigating officer that her neck scratches were sustained when she was playing with her cat. What now?

If the officers had thoroughly documented the circumstances of the investigation, they would have included B's direct statements, as well as her demeanor and any physical evidence that corroborated her account. Moreover, the officers may have kept the initial phone call as further evidentiary support for their decision to arrest A.

This poses a challenge for law enforcement since there are many defensible reasons for recantation. Oftentimes, recanted statements by a victim are not ill-intentioned, such as when they stem from the cycle of domestic violence. It would undermine public policy goals to simply arrest a victim for filing a false police report or to abandon criminal charges against a perpetrator. Many of these cases can be salvaged by comprehensively documented reports that include spontaneous statements.

A Note About "Opinions"

Law enforcement officers undergo extensive training to become skillful observers, critical thinkers, and investigators. As a result, they are often able to identify public safety information that may escape the layperson. For instance, while the significance of a particular tattoo or a particular clothing article may not spark the curiosity of the average person, officers may properly develop suspicion based on these factors as a result of their training and experience. This type of awareness is vital to a law enforcement officer's success. However, the legal ramifications of personal opinions must be carefully considered.

In their narratives, officers must explain the facts that they learn and the reasonable inferences that they glean from those facts. This includes the reasonable inferences that they make based on their training and experience. When a report contains sufficient facts and inferences, it should guide the reader to the irresistible deduction that the officer's actions, or in some cases inactions, were reasonable. For example, in a report, it would not be enough for an officer to say, "I believed Jones was drunk, so I asked him to submit to a field sobriety test." It would be much more effective to read that officer's *objective* observations of Jones. This will inform the reader, and if done properly, demonstrate that the officer's later actions were legally justified. Consider the same situation with the following description:

When I spoke with Jones, I detected a strong odor of an alcoholic beverage on his breath. He spoke in a slurred manner, and I observed that his eyes were bloodshot and watery. Based on these observations, I requested that Jones submit to a series of field sobriety tests to determine his fitness for driving.

Even though law enforcement officers are highly trained, their training alone does not qualify them as an "expert" under the rules of evidence. To qualify as an expert, an officer would require specialized or advanced training. This is not to say that officers cannot report general conclusions they reach through the deductive process. Rather, it just means that police reports require more than an officer's general opinions.

In those instances when a person has been recognized by a court as an expert witness, their opinion may be offered, but only after their credentials have been established and a proper foundation has been laid. This is often the case with law enforcement members who have obtained advanced certifications in traffic crash reconstruction, drug recognition, statement analysis, and the like.

Generally, for someone to be recognized as an *expert*, their opinions must have been formed by employing a legally accepted skill level.[2] In those cases, their "expert" opinion must comport with the legal standard requiring scientific, technical, or specialized knowledge.

Since these tend to be evidentiary decisions made by a judge, it is generally impermissible for officers to offer their opinions without sufficient foundational data. In court, this will include a rundown of the officer's qualifications, specialized training, experience, education, years of service, work assignments, and so on. When the defense is confronted with an officer who is testifying as an expert witness, the usual approach is to present an opposing expert to refute the officer's findings. This is often referred to as a "battle of the experts".

So how does all of this relate to police report writing? Remember that most investigations submitted to a prosecuting attorney begin at the patrol level. These cases find root in an agency's day-to-day operations and are constructed through the investigative efforts of the first responding officers. This includes the observations they make, the evidence they locate, the facts they assemble, and the inferences they draw. And since at its core, the legal system is an adversarial process, poorly documented investigations commonly fail.

Please take note of the words *poorly documented*. This is not synonymous with *poorly conducted*. Law enforcement officers can possess tremendous investigative skill and reach sound conclusions but have unsuccessful cases. Failing to properly articulate information ensures that result. Thorough investigations tend to be defenseless against the scrutiny brought on by poorly written police reports.

---

[2] For example, in <u>Kumho Tire Co. v. Carmichael</u>, 526 U.S. 137 (1999), the United States Supreme Court noted that scientific, technical, or specialized knowledge can "become the subject of expert testimony."

Organization and Structure

Practice, practice, practice! Any seasoned investigator will tell you that criminal investigations can take odd turns and that information can come from all directions. Many times, there is no rhyme or reason to how information is received. It can come from informants, unidentified witnesses, security cameras, documents, tiplines, physical evidence, and so on. Officers starting their careers quickly learn that when an investigation increases in complexity, so does the need for organization. With practice, the ability to sift through information and then structure it in a coherent way becomes easier.

Beyond our house analogy for structuring a police report, another helpful analogy can be made by comparing a police report to a map. We know that maps are tools used to guide you to a destination. They offer direction, but also provide perspective for a large area. When using a map, you know that there is likely more than one route to a destination. Similarly, along with alternate routes, there may be detours or hidden obstacles. Some routes are direct, while others are not.

This same logic holds true for a police report. Investigations can have a clear path that is focused and clear. Other times, an investigation may require improvisation, creating the need for adaptability. Officers must make judgment calls on which routes to take. Even though a particular track may be more direct, it could contain obstacles that should be avoided.

If the destination of a case is an arrest, the officer writing the report must describe every road taken to get there. To illustrate, we consider the following scenario:

Officer Adams was dispatched to Marty's Market for a shoplifting complaint. When he arrived at the store, the owner reported that a male suspect had stolen over \$300 worth of cigarettes. Officer Adams conducted a criminal investigation which resulted in the arrest of Fred Holmes.

Pretty clear-cut scenario, right? In this snippet, you are told the reason why Officer Adams responded to the store. You are also told of the outcome of the investigation. However, you, the reader, should have several questions about what transpired between the time that Officer Adams received the call to respond and when he arrested Holmes. In fact, as a criminal case that resulted in an arrest, this investigation has numerous questions that *need* to be answered.

Take a moment and identify some of the questions that you would want answered if you were the responding officer. Although there is no complete list, questions would include:

- **How did the owner become aware of the theft? Did he witness it? Did someone else witness it?**
- **Were any other items taken from the store?**
- **Was the suspect acting alone or was he with someone else?**
- **Was there surveillance footage of the theft? If so, did Officer Adams review it? Did he seize it for evidence?**
- **Can the store owner confirm the brand, value, and number of cartons taken? If so, how?**
- **How did Officer Adams identify Holmes as the suspect?**
- **What information provided probable cause to arrest Holmes?**
- **Where did Officer Adams find Holmes?**
- **Was Holmes in possession of the stolen cigarettes when he was found?**
- **What did Officer Adams do after finding Holmes? Did he interrogate him? If so, did he provide Holmes with his Miranda warnings?**
- **Did Holmes confess to the shoplifting?**
- **What happened after Holmes was arrested? Was he held for court? Was he released on a summons to appear? Was he presented before a bail commissioner?**

This may seem like an exhaustive list, but with practice, these types of inquiries become second nature. An organized police report will answer these basic questions since good investigations yield logical answers. Certainly, there are times when information comes from unexpected places or unapparent links are made between facts. When that happens, though, officers can describe, in a structured sense, how their decisions were affected by earlier information they uncovered. Sometimes, the information confirms investigative theories. Other times, the information dispels suspicion or serves to exclude suspects. In the above scenario, some of the investigative links might be reported as follows:

On June 18, 2022, at approximately 2230 hours, I, Officer Adams, was dispatched to Marty's Market at 123 Elm Street for a shoplifting complaint. Upon my arrival, I met with the victim, later identified as the business owner, Martin Jackson.

Jackson reported that while he was cleaning the coffee counter in the rear of the store, he observed a middle-aged white male, later identified as Fred Holmes ("Holmes") enter the store. Holmes reportedly leaned over the front counter and grabbed several cartons of Marlboro cigarettes that were located on a folding table behind the cash register.

According to Jackson, he yelled to Holmes, who then fled from the store with the cigarettes tucked under his arm. Jackson stated he was certain that Holmes did not enter a vehicle since he heard no engine and saw no headlights or brake lights.

Holmes was described by Jackson as approximately 45 years old, unshaven, with shoulder length brown hair. Holmes was also reportedly wearing a yellow sweatshirt and blue jeans. Jackson estimated that Holmes was approximately six feet tall and of average build.

Jackson inventoried the remaining cigarettes and found that six (6) cartons of Marlboro cigarettes were stolen. Each carton had a retail value of $65.00.

When I reviewed the surveillance footage provided by Jackson, I immediately recognized Holmes due to my prior contacts with him.

As you can see, a clearer picture emerges as you read through the report narrative. Detailed information is not incorporated into one oversized paragraph that bounces from topic to topic. Rather, the report utilizes separate paragraphs to explain the evolution of the case in the most linear way possible. This helps the reader comprehend the sequence of events. And while the report is generally chronological, when it must deviate back in time, it does so in a logical way.

With that said, organizing a report requires more than just separate paragraphs and chronological statements. Skilled investigators ask probing questions, and though they may have excellent memories, the information they glean must be recorded as contemporaneously as possible. This is usually in the form of field notes.

While we will discuss field notes in greater detail in Chapter 10, their general purpose is to act as a memory aid. Field notes provide officers with a means for recalling key information. That information will vary based on the type of case, but the act of detailing itself typically cements the officer's recollections of investigative developments. Officers will be well-served to utilize incident checklists when gathering field notes, especially since predetermined lists target the information that is vital to a case.

As police narratives are written, they must be organized in a way that tells the reader *an investigative story*. The typical police report is organized into identifiable sections, which we will discuss now.

The Introduction

The introductory paragraph of a police report should include the date, the time, the location of the call, the reporting officer's identity, and how or why the officer became involved. Oftentimes, the first few sentences of the report provide the bulk of this information.

On March 11, 2022, at approximately 1345 hours, I, Officer Adams, was dispatched to the intersection of Oak Street and Main Avenue for the report of a motor vehicle crash. The dispatcher advised me that the vehicles were still in the roadway, and it was unknown if any of the vehicle occupants were injured.

This information is needed to set the stage for the remainder of the police report. In this call, the information was given to the officer by a dispatcher, as opposed to the officer personally seeing the crash or locating it while on patrol. This means that the causal factors of the crash were *not* observed firsthand by the officer. Therefore, the officer must rely on information provided second or third hand.

In addition, the officer's response level will be dictated by the information given by the dispatcher. In this crash example, the severity of the motor vehicle accident is unknown, so the officer will likely use the patrol vehicle's emergency equipment to arrive quickly. The officer might find that the vehicles were moved safely into a parking lot and the occupants were unhurt. On the contrary, the crash may be serious and involve multiple injuries or significant traffic hazards. The point here is that when officers write report introductions, they are framing the remainder of the narrative and setting its tempo.

The Account

The officer's account represents the main body of the report. It is akin to the plot of a story in that it provides *the bulk of the explanatory information.* The account typically includes background information, connections between pieces of evidence, the people involved, actions taken by the officer, and so on.

A helpful approach in narrative writing is to consider the reasons for being at a scene in the first place. The starting point of a case is logically related to its conclusion, even when there are detours along the way. In this way, it is beneficial for officers to take an overarching view of the event. This will help them prioritize their tasks and reinforce the need for certain data points. In the pages that follow, you will see some general categories of information typically found in reports.

Identities of People

In police reports, it is common to see several different categories of people, such as witnesses, suspects, victims, reporting parties, bystanders, and other officers involved.

The "Statements"
Given by the People Involved

Statements here means the information that a person reports to an officer. A statement can be given by anyone involved in a case, such as the victim of the crime, a witness to an event, or the person being arrested. Likewise, statements can be in writing, provided verbally, or given demonstrably.

Descriptions of Places or Conditions

A police report may require that the investigating officer describe a physical location. Depending on the case, it could be a single location or multiple locations. These places may be public or private. At times, they may involve a specific address (i.e., 123 Main Street) or a general location (i.e., the wooded area abutting Washington Park). References in the report may also require a schematic drawing of a physical area, such as when a crime scene is sketched. Likewise, the general condition of the place observed must be documented in detail. For instance, consider the officer who responds to a child neglect complaint. It would be important for the officer to describe the condition of the home. Was the home clean or dirty? Was it cluttered? Did it have any dangerous conditions, such as exposed wires or missing stairway railings?

Descriptions of Property

Property descriptions are regularly included in police reports. Property refers to items that were stolen, seized, damaged, recovered, photographed, suspected, or simply involved. For example, a report narrative may detail the bicycle stolen from a person's shed; it may describe the vehicle impounded after the driver was arrested for operating under the influence; or it may depict the manner in which a firearm's serial number had been obliterated. Consider that personal or tangible property is often evidence in a case, even when it is indirectly related.

Look at the following example. It involves a knife that an officer observed at a crime scene. As the reader, which description gives you a better visual in your mind's eye?

When I entered the kitchen, I saw a knife with dried blood on it.

OR

When I entered the kitchen, I saw a steak knife resting on the edge of the kitchen table. The knife had a black and gray handle, and upon closer inspection, I observed that there was a reddish-brown smear on the blade, consistent with the presence of dried blood. The knife blade measured 4 inches from the tip of the blade to the start of the handle, and the blade was slightly bent.

Descriptions of Physical Injuries or Observable Physical Characteristics

We know that police officers investigate crimes and other types of events that involve people being injured or killed. In fact, the range of cases where officers investigate injury or death is exceptionally wide. Each day, police officers respond to murders, assaults, motor vehicle crashes, industrial accidents, suicides, overdoses, unattended deaths (either suspicious or non-suspicious), abuse cases, and so on.

Irrespective of modern crime scene photography and the availability of body-worn cameras, an officer's documented observations of physical injuries or a body's characteristics must be thorough and specific. Scenes can quickly change due to external conditions such as weather, fluctuating temperatures, or the inevitable impact of human contact during crime scene processing. Consequently, when scenes are first observed, they are in their purest state.

Describing physical injuries or the condition of a body can be tricky. There are differences between lacerations, bruises, abrasions, post-mortem lividity, ligature marks, decomposition, and so on. Officers must be prepared to describe specific aspects of the injury itself. This might include the size of an injury, its severity, its location, and when appropriate, whether it appeared to be a defensive or offensive wound. Here are some general examples:

- **I observed that Smith had minor swelling on the left side of his lower lip and small blood drops on the left front of his shirt.**
- **When I arrived at the scene of the motorcycle crash, I observed the driver seated on the sidewalk. He had a deep laceration to his forehead, above his right eye. The wound was approximately two inches long and was bleeding heavily.**
- **When I entered the first-floor bedroom, I observed the decedent on the floor between the bureau and the bed. I noticed there was lividity visible on his left side. Due to the positioning of the decedent's body, the signs of lividity were present primarily on the left side of his face and on the outer portion of his left arm, between his wrist and elbow.**

Observations of a Person's Actions or Behaviors

Beyond the information received from others to describe an event or condition, officers themselves will make many personal observations. And since there is an important difference between direct and indirect evidence, the origin of the information relied upon by the officer must be noted in the report. Statements from others may help fortify an officer's observations or may demonstrate a witness's or suspect's partiality. In some cases, an officer's observations are the primary evidence offered against a suspect, which is common with motor vehicle offenses, such as drunk driving cases.

Overview of the Officer's Actions

Consider these questions – why did the officer act in a certain way? Was it necessary for safety? Was it statutorily required? Was it needed to preserve evidence or keep the peace? Were there other available alternatives?

Reports are an opportunity for officers to explain their reasoning. Since case types run the gamut, an officer's responsibilities will often vary. A damaged mailbox will require fewer steps than a multi-victim investigation into cyber-harassment. Likewise, basic investigations can quickly turn into lengthy ones without warning. It should come as no surprise that the need for explanatory information in a report increases exponentially as cases become more intricate.

Example: You are patrolling your district and receive a call to respond to an armed robbery at a gas station. You learn that the cashier was stabbed during the robbery and is being transported to the hospital. Your sergeant directs you to search the area for the suspect.

While doing so, you observe a large knife resting on the ground at the edge of the station's parking lot. As a police officer, you must act, right? What will you do? Here are some questions you can ask yourself:

- **Should I notify dispatch of the weapon's location and continue my search?**
- **Should I pause my search and cordon off the area so that the evidence is not disturbed?**
- **Should I request detectives or a crime scene processing unit?**
- **Should I photograph or seize the knife?**

These questions are only a start. You must think about many additional factors, such as the resources available to you, the number of officers responding, your department's policies for evidence collection, and so on. Importantly, your actions must be reasonable and conform to law enforcement best practices. Here, the knife is likely the weapon used in a serious crime, so its potential for evidentiary value is high. It could yield DNA evidence, trace evidence, or fingerprints, so leaving it behind is not an option.

Other times, a police officer's actions are examined for their direct impact on a person. Such is the case when physical force is required, or some type of drastic action is necessary. In our system of justice, officers are given wide discretion, but their actions are always judged according to a reasonableness standard.

Relevant Connections Made Between Evidence and Other Information

A quintessential part of the fact-gathering process for police officers is that they must make logical connections between evidence and other information. Officers are responsible for identifying facts and then making inferences from those facts. Although this can sometimes be a daunting task, it can lead to powerful evidence in a criminal investigation.

Commonly, information viewed in isolation is not nearly as robust or persuasive as information viewed cumulatively. For instance, a person who has bloodshot eyes may have seasonal allergies. A person who has bloodshot eyes along with slurred speech and poor balance is likely intoxicated. Remember that in criminal law, every crime is made up of specific elements, and *all* must be present to establish that a criminal offense was committed. There is no alternative.

While the connections between evidence and other information are fundamental to the development of probable cause, which we discussed at length in Chapter 3, the importance of an officer making those connections is broader. Remember that *not all police investigations are criminal investigations*. How they evolve depends on the facts of each case. What started out as a criminal investigation may be resolved later as a civil matter. For instance, the person who claims to have been "robbed" might have simply entered into a bad contract.

In policing, there is no shortage of non-criminal events that require some form of investigation. Common examples include traffic accidents, the protective custody of a person, certain types of missing persons reports, and so on. In those cases that do not result in an arrest, the connections the officer makes between evidence and other information are just as important. For instance, these connections may:

- **Corroborate or contradict another person's account.**
- **Substantiate that an event occurred.**
- **Establish aggravating or mitigating factors in an incident.**
- **Confirm a person's involvement or non-involvement in the case.**
- **Develop information that is either exculpatory or inculpatory.**
- **Offer insight into a person's motivations.**

In criminal law, crimes do not exist without suspects having the requisite mental state. This means they must have a specific or general intent to perform certain actions prohibited by law. For example, the crime of embezzlement occurs when someone intends to steal property entrusted to them through employment or some other reason. This could be a bank teller who steals a customer's deposit or loan payment. That same bank teller would not be charged with embezzlement for stealing a cell phone from a customer's car. Although cell phone theft would still be a crime, the bank teller's responsibilities were related to financial transactions, not lot security. Consequently, the criminal charge would be different.

Relational and cumulative information is a key factor in determining the strength of a criminal investigation. Sometimes, it also creates the secondary question of "what should I do with the information I just received?"

Let's say an officer learns that a person was seen running from the scene of an arson. Is it enough for the officer to just note the information and move on? Of course not. They may need to canvass the area, broadcast the suspect's description, research similar cases, and so on. There are many times when the answers to investigative questions seem to only generate more avenues to explore.

The Conclusion

The conclusion of a police report should not be confused with the end of an investigation. The two are *not* synonymous. While the conclusion of an officer's report *may* represent the end of a case, it is often a statement of how *that officer's involvement* concluded.

There are several outcomes. A case may be closed when an officer makes an arrest or determines that the matter is not a criminal offense. The officer may note that a case requires additional investigation. Other times, the officer may need to get other divisions involved. Depending on the size of the police agency, an officer's responsibilities in an investigation will vary.

Smaller agencies may require that officers follow their cases until the end. Larger agencies may utilize specialty units to provide investigative support. Sometimes, complex investigations trigger the need for assistance from larger agencies, such as when the state police or local sheriff's office are called in for major crime scenes. A report's conclusion may simply describe the transfer of jurisdiction in a case.

Moreover, there may be state or federal agencies that are better equipped for investigations, such as departments of elderly affairs, departments of children and families, or the United States Secret Service for matters involving counterfeiting of United States currency.

Here are some examples of ways that officers may conclude their reports. This is not a complete list, but rather it provides representative samples for you to consider.

Report Conclusion Examples	Examples Explained
"This case was suspended pending further information."	Typically, an investigation will be suspended when all investigative leads are exhausted. This is common with investigations classified as "cold cases."
"Smith stated that she did not want to press charges against Johnson for damaging her vehicle. Johnson agreed to pay for all repairs and the case was closed at the request of Smith."	When a witness or victim declines to file a complaint, the case may be closed unless there is specific reason to continue the investigation. Most cases are instituted or withdrawn at the request of a victim. There are times, though, when officers have a statutory obligation to act regardless of the victim's wishes (i.e., domestic violence offenses, matters involving elderly or child victims).
"I forwarded the case to the Detective Division for further investigation."	Most larger agencies have specialty units that are called in for more complex investigations. Typically, these units take primary responsibility for serious cases, such as those involving violent crimes (i.e., murder, weapons offenses, sexual assaults, child abuse reports), or offenses that require specialized skill or training to investigate, such as cybercrime, the manufacture or distribution of drugs, or traffic crash reconstruction.

Report Conclusion Examples	Examples Explained
"I arrested Greene for one count of larceny. I placed him in handcuffs that were doubled-locked and checked for tightness and then transported him to police headquarters. There, I turned Greene over to Officer Jones for processing and booking. Later, Greene was released on a summons to appear in district court."	An officer's involvement in a case may end when an arrestee is turned over to a booking officer or jailer. Prisoners are usually photographed, fingerprinted, and in some cases, given a buccal swab. Later, they may be released on a summons, held for the next session of court, or transferred to another jail or holding facility.
"Based on the investigation, this matter was determined to be a civil dispute and no criminal charges were warranted against either party."	This conclusion is commonly reached when an investigation finds that the facts and circumstances did not meet the threshold for a criminal offense. The distinctions between a crime and a civil matter can be subtle, and some investigation is usually required to make a proper determination. Recall that criminal offenses are made up of specific elements that must be met.
"The investigation will continue."	Here, the officer is delaying further investigation until a later time. It is different than suspending an investigation entirely. Usually, the officer continues to carry the case as an active one since investigative avenues are still known, likely, or possible. Sometimes, a more serious case has taken precedence, or the officer is awaiting lab results or a response from a person involved in the investigation.

As with evidentiary chains of custody, investigations must travel logical and definitive routes. Whether investigations are suspended, solved, closed, continued, or forwarded, the routes they take must be described in the report's conclusion. Because every report is meant to inform others, officers must not only document their specific role in a case, but also explain where that case stands at the time of the report.

Summary

Police reports are very consequential, so they must be composed in an understandable way. Remember that reports tell the factual "story" of an investigation. They are not written for entertainment value, and there is no audience in the theatrical sense. Instead, reports are designed to memorialize the facts and circumstances of a case, whether or not that case involves a minor or major crime, a civil matter, or some other type of event.

Time and again, the most effective reports are those written in a structured way. Narratives that are well-organized allow the reader to better grasp the evolution of a case, and linear accounts provide clear and comprehensible paths. As you read more narratives, you will see that when reports are structured, they are more easily digested by the reader. Likewise, the information provided in a police report must always remain objective.

Chapter 5
The Dos and Don'ts of Narrative Writing

As is common with police operations, local practices and agency policy will dictate the way reports are written. What follows are some general approaches to police reporting and the reasons why they are recommended.

Do: Use First Person

With police reporting, the current trend is for officers to write their reports in first-person. When you have the opportunity to read reports in bulk, you will see that the use of first person in a narrative makes sense. It allows the reporting officer to speak directly to the reader using the pronouns "I" and "we." These types of reports are easy to identify.

In years past, many law enforcement officers were trained to write their narratives from a third person point of view. This narrative approach sounds unnatural, mainly because officers speak about themselves as if watching an event from a distance. Common for police reports written in third person is the use of pronouns such as "he," "she," and "they."

Compare the following statements written in first person and third person:

Example 1

- *First Person.* **When I arrived on scene, I saw Jones seated on the metal guardrail next to a red Ford Mustang.**

OR

- *Third Person.* **When Sergeant Smith arrived on scene, he saw Jones seated on the metal guardrail next to a red Ford Mustang.**

Example 2

- ***First Person.*** **After Jones failed a series of standardized field sobriety tests, I determined that he was unfit to safely operate a motor vehicle.**

OR

- ***Third Person.*** **After Jones failed a series of standardized field sobriety tests, Sergeant Smith determined that he was unfit to safely operate a motor vehicle.**

Notice the distinct differences in the officer's statements in each of these examples. You can see that the first-person point of view presents the author as a participant while the third person takes the point of view of a bystander. When you consider that Sergeant Smith is talking about himself, the report narrative seems odd and imprecise.

Since you are reading this book, you understand that police officers should always do their best to write clear and effective narratives. Beyond the unnatural feelings that are associated with third person reports, first person accounts alleviate muddled language by *avoiding pronoun confusion in narratives.* Read the above third person example again and pay close attention to the pronoun. While you can discern what was *intended* by the writer (i.e., Jones was unfit to drive), can you also see that this statement can be construed as Sergeant Smith declaring *himself* to be the one unfit? Look at it closely. This type of ambiguity can be quickly capitalized upon by an astute defense attorney.

Police reports can, and often do, involve many people. Throughout this book, we have discussed several of them, such as witnesses, victims, suspects, reporting parties, and involved persons. There is no need to inject uncertainty into a narrative by distorting the essential connections between people and facts. Remember that pronouns like "he," "she," and "they" in a report will refer to any number of people, while "I" will refer to *only one.*

First Person Personalizes
the Officer's Account

For many of the same reasons stated above, police officers should personalize their narratives. Think about it. When officers speak directly to the reader, they give a candid view from their own vantage point. Since most people are not trained in law enforcement practices and procedures, the reasoning behind a particular action may escape the layperson. A personalized approach to writing offers the chance to say to the reader "given the circumstances that I faced at the time, this is why I did what I did."

- ***First person.*** **As I turned towards my cruiser, the suspect quickly lunged for my firearm. I feared for my safety and struck the suspect with my right elbow to create distance between us.**

OR

- ***Third Person.*** **As Officer Adams turned towards his cruiser, the suspect quickly lunged for his firearm. Officer Adams feared for his safety and used an elbow strike to create distance between them.**

Third person places the officer, and consequently the reader, on the outside of an event. This serves to distance the reader from the circumstances the officer faced and, unfortunately, may soften the true gravity of the incident itself. Unwarranted doubt about an officer's split-second decisions can be formed simply because the magnitude of the event was not communicated effectively.

In this example, note also that there is pronoun confusion created using third person. Did the suspect grab his own firearm or did he lunge for the officer's gun? If ever a case needs to have all of its lingering questions answered, it is one that involves the use of physical force.

First Person Is a Direct Form of Writing That Enhances an Officer's Credibility

When officers take ownership of the decisions they make, they lend more credibility. First person is the officer speaking directly to the reader. There is no hidden subtext. It is a powerful approach to reporting because information is provided in a straightforward manner.

A police narrative written in an indirect way, whether intentionally or not, will likely raise questions. This should not come as a surprise. Every day, techniques are used to analyze and interpret a person's statement, such as statement analysis or scientific content analysis. Those who seek to distance themselves from their own words or actions usually do so for a reason, which a perceptive investigator will see as an investigative red flag. The same principles apply to narrative writing.

While our discussion here may seem to be a deeper dive into narrative writing than one might expect, the impact of indirect reporting must be considered. Analyzing a person's statements comes down to a search for subtext in language. Words or phrases can be examined for hidden truths or may demonstrate subtle falsities. And this matters in report writing because a third person point of view may feed the argument that *the officer is attempting to create distance from what they did.*

If a report generates questions about police action, or if it creates concerns about police motives, the entire investigation can be derailed. Unfortunately, disruptions in cases can occur even if the questions raised are misleading or inaccurate. Policing is a complex field that generates public interest – and consequently, scrutiny. Decisions, especially those in high profile cases, are routinely examined. Think of how many news headlines you see each day that involve crime and policing. When an officer describes their actions in the first person – from their point of view – they are declaring that their decisions are their own.

Do: Use Active Voice

In general, active voice in a police report minimizes wordiness and contributes to the report's overall clarity. Like the use of first person, active voice ensures that the officer's narrative is more direct and concise. Passive voice as a rule of grammar just means that the subject of the sentence is performing the action. Here are a few examples.

- *Active voice.* **I escorted John Smith into the cellblock.**
- *Passive voice.* **John Smith was escorted into the cellblock by me.**

OR

- *Active voice.* **I advised Derry of his Miranda warnings.**
- *Passive voice.* **Derry was advised of his Miranda warnings by me.**

At times, passive voice may be acceptable in a police report. This commonly occurs when the officer writing the report seeks to emphasize what received the action.

Don't: Use Question-and-Answer Format

It is an interesting irony that officers are trained to ask questions but should generally avoid writing their narratives in question-and-answer format. It almost seems counterintuitive. While there are some notable exceptions, the majority of police reports should be written in summation form as opposed to dialogue form. The product is a police report that is easier to follow and understand.

To highlight this, consider a basic scenario. You responded to a fight and made some observations. Based on what you saw, you asked certain people questions. The answers you received led you to a suspect. You later arrested him. Case closed. Your report will document this process and detail the investigation as it unfolded. In doing so, you will answer the important questions of "who, what, where, when, why, and how?"

Your summary, although comprehensive, should not be a verbatim account of each question you asked and each answer you received. It could not be. Time would not permit it, your efficiency would suffer, and your overall effectiveness would decline. A police department's operations would grind to a halt if that level of agonizing specificity were required.

This is a truism consistent across many fields. For instance, when judges draft legal decisions, they do not recount every word argued by opposing attorneys and every word uttered by witnesses. Rather, they consider the arguments made, the testimony given, and the evidence presented when reaching their decisions. They draft their legal opinions based on these factors in conjunction with legal precedent, reasonable conclusions, and their experience. If there was a particularly influential point made during a hearing, the judge may directly mention it. But the bulk of the information is synthesized.

The same is true with police reporting. By and large, your narrative should provide the reader with a detailed overview of what you encountered, without a word for word re-enactment. Take a look at the following examples:

When I arrived on scene, I met with Andrews, who was the only known witness to the crash. Andrews reported that he saw an older model, red, four-door sedan driving south on Main Avenue, away from the accident scene. Although he was unsure of the registration plate or number of occupants, he stated that he believed the sedan was a Ford.

If this same account was provided in a question-and-answer format, it would read something like this:

When I arrived on scene, I met with Andrews, who was the only known witness to the crash. I asked Andrews if he saw any vehicles leaving the accident scene. He said that he did. I asked him if he could describe the fleeing vehicle. Andrews said it was an older model, red, four door sedan. I also asked him in which direction the vehicle fled. He said it drove south on Main Avenue, away from the accident scene. I then asked Andrews if he was able to view the vehicle's registration plate. He indicated that he was not. I next asked him if he knew the make of the vehicle or if he could tell how many occupants were in it. Andrews said that he thought it was a Ford.

As you can see, the second paragraph provides the reader with the same information but requires more than twice as many words to do so. And, even though it is wordier, it is not necessarily more detailed. Instead, the second paragraph lacks the clarity of the first and frustrates the reader with its volley of information.

With that said, remember that certain statements, such as spontaneous utterances, operate as an exception to the hearsay rule. Therefore, if a quoted statement is material to a case, it rightly belongs in the narrative. Unplanned, extemporaneous statements can be powerful evidence and need not be paraphrased. For example, imagine you are investigating a vandalized windshield. You stop someone running from the area and, without prompting, the person yells, "I didn't break any windows." While this statement may not be a full admission, it does have considerable evidentiary value. Notably, it suggests a guilty conscience on the part of the speaker.

While the question-and-answer format should generally be avoided, it is fitting for reports that document key interviews or interrogations in serious cases. There, verbatim responses are useful to verify information, test a suspect's credibility, or find subtext. Sequences of events and small pieces of information can be invaluable when assembling investigative timelines or corroborating details. Likewise, interrogations of people suspected of serious crimes, such as murder or sexual assault, will usually be audio and video recorded.

As with many aspects of police report writing, though, agency policy and local practice will provide direction. There may be additional situations where the question and answer format is acceptable or desirable. However, the general rule for everyday police reports is that narratives should be written in a detailed, summary form.

Do: Use Past Tense

By virtue of the fact that you are writing a police report – that is, documenting information that you *learned* during your investigation – you are referencing *past* events. For instance, the officer who responded to a domestic dispute and confirmed that a battery took place will later write a narrative to memorialize that *earlier* event. This is the nature of being a law enforcement officer. Respond. Act. Document.

Over time, past tense has become the preferred, more precise approach to writing reports. Since accuracy can be elusive with subtle changes in language, the use of past tense has proven to be the most effective way to communicate information. Consider the following example.

- **Mary Jones enters the kitchen, and her husband John punches her in the face with his right fist. He chokes her by gripping the front of her neck with both of his hands and she is unable to break free.**

OR

- **Mary Jones reported that after she entered the kitchen, her husband John punched her in the face with his right fist. She said that he then choked her by gripping the front of her neck with both of his hands and she was unable to break free.**

Both paint a similar picture of the incident, right?

Although these two accounts are *consistent*, they are not the *same*. The first example reads as if the officer is watching the incident unfold but is *failing to act*. While we know this is not the case, the mere fact that it creates an inaccurate picture brings to light that the report is flawed. It would be unlikely that an officer would observe an unfolding crime and simultaneously write about it without taking action. However, present tense creates this illusion because information is represented as firsthand knowledge. The difference is subtle, but there *is* a difference.

One helpful method for effectively using past tense is to view investigations in a linear way. As cases proceed, additional facts are uncovered. Those newly learned facts build upon earlier pieces of information, which sharpens an investigation's focus. This natural evolution cannot be accomplished in a meaningful way if an officer mistakenly reports events in real time. Present tense narratives can confuse or disrupt the flow of information, especially when *past* factors prompt *later* decisions.

Of course, since all general rules have exceptions, there are instances when an unavoidable shift in verb tense from past to present improves accuracy. When this occurs, it tends to fall into one of two areas:

1. *You are describing a condition that is still in existence, such as a physical location or an unchanging characteristic.*

   - **I responded to 12 Elm Street for a domestic disturbance. The building *is* a multi-unit apartment complex with two floors.**

- **Upon our arrival at headquarters, I escorted Jones into the cell block holding room. This room *is* both audio and video recorded.**

2. *It adds qualifying information that is not yet known, completed, or available.*

- **As of this report, I *am* awaiting toxicology test results from the state crime laboratory.**
- **There are no known suspects at *this* time.**
- **I *will* follow up with Jack Jones during my next shift on October 10, 2022.**
- **This case *is* suspended pending any further leads.**

Summary

The dos and don'ts of narrative writing discussed in this chapter will assist you in composing quality police reports. In truth, some of the aspects we have covered here are subtle or technical distinctions in language. It is always important to remember that minor changes in word choice can result in entirely different perceptions of the same event. If your goal is to write clear and accurate reports, a better understanding of the writing styles that introduce ambiguity or inaccuracy into a narrative will be of great help.

Chapter 6
Types of Law Enforcement Reports

Every police department must meet certain reporting requirements. Commonly, departments track domestic violence incidents, uses of force, motor vehicle crashes, crime trends, and so on. As police departments have become more computer based, the market for public safety software programs has expanded. Typically, these systems can be used to categorize police events while offering a host of tools to research and classify them by time, place, and type. In this chapter, we will discuss some of the common categories that are used.

Recall from Chapter 2 that operational reports represent the majority of police reports taken at the patrol level. These, as you know, differ from the administrative reports typically required of command staff or supervisors. Our focus here will not be on administrative topics. Those are better suited for first-line supervision or police management courses. The average patrol officer will not be required to submit budget reports, conduct internal affairs investigations, or give crime analysis presentations.

Instead, patrol officers must become accustomed to operational reporting requirements. In modern policing, these requirements have increased for several reasons, ranging from enhanced transparency to public awareness.

At the patrol level, police reports are commonly broken down into the following broad categories:

- **Case Reports (sometimes called Incident Reports, Case Reports or Offense Reports).**
- **Field Interview Reports (sometimes called Field Investigation Reports or "Stop and Chats").**
- **Accident Reports (sometimes called Crash Reports).**
- **Arrest Reports.**

Although we will discuss each report type, I encourage you to refer to your agency's local policies for reporting information.

Case Reports

Your agency may refer to this type of report as a case report, offense report, crime report, or an incident report. For ease here, we will just refer to them as case reports.

The case report is the most common report taken by officers. By default, most investigations that do not involve an arrest, motor vehicle crash, or limited interview will fall into this category. Case reports are a mechanism for documenting crimes (or suspected crimes) *before* they are solved, or if solved, before an arrest is made. They also document a wide range of situations that do not fit neatly into a box, such as when an official record of an event is advisable. Examples include contentious civil matters, community policing events, or public hazards.

As discussed in Chapter 2, a written or computerized record of each police encounter will be made in your department's computer aided dispatch (CAD) system. Entries of this type are made when a police officer responds to a call or self-initiates some type of service activity. When an officer decides that a call requires a full report – that is, information documented beyond the simple CAD entry – the result is a case report.

Okay, so What Are Some of the Common Reasons That Officers Will Take Case Reports?

What follows is a sampling of situations or events that tend to require a police case report.

- **An officer investigates an attempted, completed, or suspected crime, regardless of whether a suspect has been identified.**
- **A police officer forces entry into a home, building or other private or public property (i.e., exigency, to execute a search or arrest warrant).**
- **A missing person is reported or located.**
- **A person is taken into protective custody or is subject to emergency commitment to a medical, substance abuse, or psychiatric facility.**

- **A police department assists another agency. This is common with mutual aid responses or the deployment of the incident command system.**
- **A death is reported, and a police response is required. Aside from deaths that involve suspicious circumstances, officers will also respond to traffic fatalities, overdoses, suicides, and a host of other death scenes.**
- **An animal bites a human.**
- **A police officer uses force in a non-arrest situation, regardless of whether an injury occurs.**
- **To document complex or potentially incendiary events that require a police response. Examples can be labor strikes, protests, and large public gatherings.**
- **When an officer believes that a case report is warranted or advisable.**
- **When an officer is directed to take a case report by a superior officer.**

Importantly, police case reports provide the written foundation for many criminal investigations. This type of report is used to document the initial stages of the officer's involvement in a case, while offering a means to categorize and catalog historical information. If you can imagine it, there is probably a justifiable reason for an officer to complete a case report.

But Is It That Complicated?

The decision to complete a full police case report is frequently left to the discretion of the investigating officer. Barring mandatory reporting, officers will often need to make judgment calls regarding when it is advisable to pull a report. Their decision will likely rest on their agency's policies, their experience in the field, or the severity of the event. All told, police case reports answer many later questions, *so when in doubt, it is best to err on the side of caution and document the facts and circumstances you have determined.*

It sounds strange to say that the decision of whether to write a police case report can sometimes be a difficult one to make. Report writing, as evidenced by this book, is an important part of policing. However, it is not feasible or necessary to take a full police report at every event. Judgment calls must be made simply because reporting can be time-consuming and not all calls are created equally.

If officers were to take a full case report for every call, efficiency would suffer, and responsiveness would grind to a halt. It is not uncommon for small police agencies with fewer than ten police officers to receive thousands of calls for service each year. As a result, it is simply not possible to take a case report for each request. Contrasted with this, however, is the need for officers to be diligent in reporting when circumstances dictate that it is appropriate to do so.

We will consider some examples of how this will look in practice. At the outset, though, we must recognize that the average day of police work will likely not be filled with high profile crimes. Contrary to popular belief, every police shift does not involve a high-speed car chase or a murder. While these situations do occur, and officers must be ready for when they do, it would be entirely misleading to suggest that officers will not respond to their share of routine or mundane situations during the average shift.

What follows is a chart intended to give you some information to consider. Imagine that you are working the 4:00 p.m. to 12:00 a.m. shift and you respond to each of the calls listed. We know that the sheer variety of police calls can never be reduced to a single list, so we will look at a sprinkle of some common call types.

Of the following calls, which would you document in a full police case report? Which do you think would only require a CAD entry? In each instance, think about the significance of the event or the ramifications of not taking a report. To assist you, I have included some general questions you might consider as you make your decision. Later, we will review them together. By no means do these situations incorporate every variable. You must always consider the circumstances *in their totality* and remember that guidance from a supervisor is always encouraged.

Call Type	Response	Questions and Other Considerations
Check the condition. An anonymous caller reports that a panhandler is approaching cars at a major intersection and is disrupting traffic.	You respond and do not see any panhandlers present. You observe the intersection for a few moments and determine that traffic is flowing normally. You clear the area.	• Have you or other officers responded there before? • Does this call represent an ongoing problem in your community or is this an isolated request? • Have there been traffic crashes related to panhandling at this or other intersections? • Is there any evidence that someone had been present, such as handwritten signs, food containers, or other discarded items?
Dog bite. Staff at a local walk-in medical center report that a child is being treated for a minor dog bite.	Your investigation reveals that the child was bitten by his family's dog. The bite occurred within your jurisdiction. You learn that the child requires three stitches and that the dog is up to date on its vaccinations.	• Does your agency, municipality, or state require written reports for animal bites? • Are there quarantine requirements for domesticated animals that bite humans? • Will the case require a follow-up visit from an animal control officer or other agency?
Found property. A loose plastic bag of a substance believed to be an illicit drug is located by a person hiking in a local park.	You meet with the reporting person who directs you to the area where she observed the bag. Based on your training and experience, you suspect that the substance is cocaine. You conduct a search of the immediate area and observe several used syringes.	• Is this an area frequented by persons known to use or sell drugs? • Does the substance create a danger of exposure to anyone? • Can the substance be seized in a safe manner, or will it require a specialty unit? • Once seized, will this substance undergo toxicology testing, kept as evidence, or destroyed? • Is there a way to determine who left the substance behind (i.e., witnesses, surveillance cameras)?

Call Type	Response	Questions and Other Considerations
Returned missing person. The parents of sixteen-year-old Jane Smith call to report that Smith returned home. She was reported missing two days prior when she failed to return home after school. At the time of the initial report, Smith was entered into the National Crime Information Center (NCIC) database as a missing juvenile.	You confirm that Smith returned home and that she spent the prior two evenings at her friend's house. When you speak to her individually, Smith alludes to two instances of physical abuse by her father and shows you bruising on her legs. Smith's father denies the allegations. Her mother states that Smith is known to embellish facts and believes that Smith's bruises were sustained while skateboarding.	• Once located, missing persons previously entered into the NCIC database must be removed ("located"). • Do you think that the circumstances of Smith's departure were suspicious? • Are you concerned about the bruises? How about the reasons offered by Smith's parents? • Do you need to take other steps to investigate Smith's care or her home conditions? • Does the evidence demonstrate that Smith was abused? • Will another agency, such as Child Protective Services, need to be contacted?

While there is no right or wrong answer to each of these calls, here are a few additional notes that may assist you as you contemplate what your decisions would be.

- *"Check the condition" call.* This scenario would generally not require full police case report. As the responding officer, you confirmed that no one was present and determined that traffic was flowing normally. Barring a specific investigative reason for doing so, this type of call would not necessarily require more than a CAD entry.
- *"Dog bite" call.* This type of call typically requires a full case report. Given the need for independent verification of vaccination records and the potential for violations, follow-up is essential. Most jurisdictions have enacted laws, ordinances, or local rules dealing with animal bites and animal licensing. These often require a quarantine period for the animal involved and/or a viciousness hearing. If your agency employs animal control officers, you will likely need to involve them.
- *"Found property" call.* This call would likely require a full incident report. Whenever an illicit drug is seized, the circumstances

surrounding the seizure should be specifically described. There are many reasons for this, such as chain of custody requirements, public health and safety considerations, and investigative needs. Likewise, it is very important to document the disposal of illicit substances.

- *"Missing person" call.* This is another example of a service call that will require a full case report. In this scenario, Smith must be removed from the NCIC database after her return is confirmed. Next, officers must do their best to verify that the child has not been abused, endangered, victimized, or involved in a criminal offense. The call in this example is further complicated by the missing juvenile's allegations of physical abuse by her father. These allegations may be true, untrue, inflated, or there may be insufficient information to make an immediate determination. As a result, the officer must conduct a thorough investigation to reach a reasonable and informed decision about whether further action is warranted.

And There's More?

Increased experience and continued training expand an officer's understanding of when and how to act. These scenarios are intended to demonstrate the importance of considering, prioritizing, and synthesizing information.

Unfortunately, many report writing courses over the years have focused too heavily on the rules of grammar. While the ability to write properly is important for overall success in policing, writing ability alone does not win the day. Beyond mechanics, narrative construction involves decision-making, professional knowledge, situational awareness, and an understanding of best practices. *Learning how to write must start with learning what to write.*

In many ways, the term "report writing" is a bit of a misnomer. Reports are the primary vehicle for documenting police *investigations.* Every case starts and ends with officers using their five senses to make determinations.

Field Interview Reports

A field interview report is generally considered a brief, informal report. These types of reports are limited in scope and their typical use is for basic intelligence gathering. Most often, field interviews are conducted as a function of patrol or detective work.

Think of field interview reports as valuable investigative tools. They document the presence of a person in a specific place at a particular time. The information that officers learn can later be cross-referenced, and sometimes provides useful clues in seemingly unconnected investigations. Here is an example.

Officer Adams is on patrol at 0330 hours and sees two men congregating in a poorly lit motel parking lot. Officer Adams speaks with the males and conducts a brief interview. She documents this interaction in a field interview report. Later that morning, several patrons of the motel report that their vehicles were vandalized with yellow spray paint.

You may ask "Were the two men involved?" If not, did they witness anyone vandalize the vehicles?

In either case, the information recorded in Officer Adams' field interview report can be helpful to a follow-up investigator. Imagine that a detective later contacts the men and learns that one of them has useful information. The man tells the detective that he saw a carload of teenagers' speed through the lot at 0400 hours, and he jotted down the car's registration plate. The detective later tracks the vehicle down and observes a can of yellow spray paint resting on the back seat. Here, the field interview yielded helpful information for the investigation.

Good field interview reports can provide investigators with a wealth of useful information. Their effectiveness over time has made them a staple in the law enforcement profession.

Accident (Crash) Reports

Accident (crash) investigations are conducted when a motor vehicle collides with another vehicle, a stationary object, an animal, or a pedestrian. Most states *require* that police officers complete a motor vehicle accident report when personal injury or physical damage results from a crash. Accident reports are very common for police officers, and there is considerable time spent at the police academy teaching recruits about basic crash investigations.

Usually, an accident report consists of (1) a crash narrative, (2) a fillable form noting the specific details and conditions of the crash, and (3) a sketch of the scene. Fillable accident forms operate as a detailed checklist and serve as an excellent organizational tool for investigations. Typical categories on fillable accident report forms are:

- **Date, time, and location of the crash.**
- **The vehicles or property involved.**
- **The people involved. These would include operators, vehicle or property owners, lessees, passengers, witnesses, pedestrians, and investigators.**
- **Safety information, such as seat belt use, airbag deployment, child restraint seat use.**
- **Insurance information.**
- **Weather, road, lighting, and traffic conditions.**
- **The presence or absence of traffic control devices.**
- **Specific crash factors. Some examples are pre-crash vehicle movements, directions of travel, speed limits, manners of collision, driver distractions, and evidence of substance use.**
- **Tow company information.**
- **Injuries reported and treatment received (i.e., hospital transport, on-scene medical assessment).**
- **The extent of vehicle or non-vehicle property damage.**
- **Crash diagrams.**
- **Witness statements.**

Traffic crash investigations yield important reportable information. For instance, an officer may determine that one of the drivers caused the crash by violating a state traffic law (such as speeding) or a criminal statute (such as reckless driving). Specifically, the narrative section provides officers with an opportunity to tie their investigative findings together. Some of the conditions that officers describe in the narrative section are:

- **Their observations of the scene (i.e., skid marks).**
- **Contributory environmental factors, such as sun glare or icy roads.**
- **Steps taken. Officers may render aid to an injured person, call for additional resources, set up traffic cones, and so on.**

- **Status checks of the vehicles and operators through the state's registry of motor vehicles.**
- **Attempts to locate or interview witnesses.**
- **Searches for evidence related to the crash.**
- **Actions to mitigate hazards created by the crash (i.e., fluid leakage onto the road, downed wires, or broken glass).**

States have specific requirements for when and how traffic accidents are reported. Your agency will provide you with its policy, along with any statutory requirements. The narrative section, however, continues to follow the general principles of report writing.

Arrest Reports

The authority to arrest a person is an exceptional power. It is bestowed upon police officers by law, and generally originates in state or federal statutes. The extensive training that officers receive in criminal procedure is due in large part to the legal and ethical implications of possessing arrest powers. To become an effective and successful police officer, recruits must fully comprehend the scope of their authority as well as the limits of that authority.

Consider this simple statement: *A lawful arrest is a proper exercise of an officer's vested authority.* The corollary of this statement, of course, is that an unlawful arrest is an improper exercise of that authority. It's a basic premise, right? In other words, you need a lawful reason to arrest someone.

Every day in the United States, civil lawsuits and criminal actions are filed against police officers. Common allegations include civil rights violations, intentional torts, and claims of criminal conduct, such as assault and battery. Successful cases can deeply impact the officers involved, their agencies, and the entirety of the policing profession.

As with any legal action, some cases have merit, and some do not. There is a vetting process that occurs prior to trial, and while the search for truth can be inspiring, there are times when municipal choices are made strategically. For example, the decision to settle a law enforcement suit may become more of a business judgment than an acknowledgement of impropriety. In an action against a police officer, a municipality may determine that the monetary costs involved in defending a suit outweigh the costs of settlement. Routinely, these decisions begin with report reviews. Poorly written narratives can act as ammunition against officers and their agencies. For those who have experienced this reality, it can be discouraging.

So how do you avoid this? For starters, the legal justifications for making an arrest must be clearly articulated in the narrative. There should be no room for the reader to speculate about the circumstances that the officer faced. Many generations of police officers have learned the adage, *"If it is not in the report, it didn't happen"* for a reason. It is imperative that officers fully understand the importance this time-tested lesson.

One notable challenge in documenting an arrest is articulating when the probable cause line is crossed. Sometimes the authority to arrest is unmistakable, such as when an officer observes a suspect committing a crime or when the person to be arrested has a warrant issued against them. Other times, finding that line requires a judgment call based on common sense and reason. In every case, the circumstantial subtleties observed by the officer must be considered.

States, of course, will vary in how they define a police officer's arrest powers. I recommend that you defer to your academy training or consult your local laws for guidance. Typical statutes lay out the general parameters for an officer's arrest authority and will usually separately consider misdemeanor and felony cases. For example, in Rhode Island, the statute that defines an officer's arrest powers for non-felony cases notes:

A [police] officer may, without a warrant, arrest a person if the officer has reasonable cause to believe that the person is committing or has committed a misdemeanor or a petty misdemeanor, and the officer has reasonable ground to believe that person cannot be arrested later or may cause injury to himself or herself or others or loss or damage to property unless immediately arrested.

We again confront the pesky truism that the devil is in the details. Since, by their very nature, arrest reports are so closely aligned with a person's liberty interest, the failure to clearly explain the details surrounding an arrest can result in a wide range of outcomes, to include:

- **Case dismissals.**

- **Internal investigations.**
- **Citizens' complaints.**
- **Civil lawsuits.**
- **Criminal charges.**
- **Reputational harm.**

Each day, the criminal justice system weathers an inherent tug between the responsibilities of the prosecution and those of the defense. Both occupy competing roles, and this is on full display in criminal cases.

A prosecutor will face onerous legal obstacles if they seek to have evidence introduced at trial that was not properly documented by an officer. Many times, an astute defense attorney can successfully argue against the admissibility of evidence when there is scant information surrounding its seizure. This is a critical juncture in the criminal justice system, and the cumulative nature of investigations is heavily tested. For example, the officer who failed to describe what justified an interior search of a car may see the stolen firearm located during that search suppressed from the case.

Even when a defense attorney is unable to persuade a judge to suppress testimony or evidence, there are many legal arguments to be made on behalf of a defendant. Consider these challenges from a defense lawyer:

- **"Officer, if the information you testified to was so important, why didn't you include it in your police report?"**
- **"Members of the jury, if the officer's failure to report this important information was, as he testified, 'an honest mistake,' then what other 'honest mistakes' did he make during this investigation?"**
- **"Your honor, how can this officer expect the court to believe that she was diligent in her investigation when she failed to include this 'very important information' that she is now testifying to in her police report?"**
- **"Your honor, how can the prosecution argue that this information is relevant when the officer himself didn't even think it was relevant enough to include in his police report."**

Arguments such as these can hinder a case's success while calling into question the competence or diligence of the officer. Yet, while by no means complementary, these allegations pale in comparison to some of the more malignant ones that can be made against an officer.

Unfortunately, officers who fail to document key information in their reports open the door to personal attacks on their integrity. In some cases, especially when there is a lot at stake for a defendant, officers may face intense opposition. Those who try to testify to facts beyond their police reports can be met with insinuations – or even outright allegations – that their testimony was fabricated to justify criminal charges or manufactured to strengthen a weaker case.

The best solution, as we know, is to construct comprehensive narratives. When writing their arrest reports, officers must describe each material fact – both exculpatory and inculpatory – along with the investigative advancements they made. This will include legal considerations, such as crime elements, as well as procedural obligations. Whether that means logging the time that Miranda warnings were read or explaining how an exception to the warrant requirement applied, information is key.

As officers gain experience, their ability to identify and prioritize vital information is continually refined. Here are some basic considerations that can be helpful for officers when navigating some of their primary responsibilities:

- **The differences between reasonable suspicion and probable cause. A good grasp of these concepts will help officers understand when it is appropriate to stop, detain, arrest, or search.**
- **The common criminal offenses encountered by their agency (i.e., highly commercial areas yielding theft-based offenses), and the specific crime elements of these offenses.**
- **The differences between discretionary and non-discretionary uses of authority. For instance, some crimes require a formal complaint from a victim, while others, such as domestic violence crimes, do not.**
- **The differences between interviews and interrogations.**

The Importance of Arrest Reports

An arrest report holds a distinct place in the criminal justice world. It is the primary tool used by officers to describe their reasons for formally charging a suspect.

Beyond those instances when a person is immediately released on scene with a summons, a formal charge against a person will result in some loss of freedom. This may be for a temporary period at a police station, or it may result in extensive pre-trial confinement.

For example, if Jones is detained for misdemeanor shoplifting, he may be arrested and transported to the police station. Generally, he would be photographed, fingerprinted, and if there were no outstanding charges, he would likely be released pending a hearing in court. This entire process is relatively brief and would result in a limited period of confinement. However, if we modify these facts, and Jones is instead arrested for first degree robbery and held without bail, he faces a much longer period of confinement.

Of importance here is that in *both* instances, Jones has forfeited his personal liberty. It is only the length of his confinement that differs.

Moving On

As the legal threshold for making an arrest, probable cause requires that *each* element of a statutorily defined crime be established through reliable evidence. So how do we know *when* this legal obligation has been met?

To better understand what is meant by crime elements, or *corpus delicti*, it is helpful to review some representative examples. In the next section, we will take a closer look at ways an officer can document the elements of a crime in a police report. These generally fall into two categories: instances when a suspect is arrested at the scene and those when charges are warranted, but the suspect has not yet been apprehended.

Crime Elements in Police Reports

Crime elements are legally prescribed factors that must be established, either expressly or impliedly, for criminal charges to be appropriate. Without getting too deeply into the technicalities of criminal law, note that unless an officer can show that each of a crime's defined elements has been met, that crime has not been committed. It is that simple. It does not matter if some, or even most, of the crime's elements are present. *It is legally impossible for a crime to have occurred when one of its elements is missing.*

Think of a car's engine. If every component is present and working properly, the engine will function. If, however, a major component of the engine is missing, or defective, it will fail. It would not matter if the other components were pristine. The same is true with criminal charges. No case will succeed in the criminal justice system when it lacks evidence to support each of a crime's elements.

Establishing crime elements through evidence. As you uncover information during an investigation, remember that evidence can take many forms. It can be direct evidence, such as eyewitness testimony, camera footage, or ballistics testing. It can also take the form of circumstantial, or indirect evidence, borne out of logical connections and reasonable inferences.

Famed attorney Vincent Bugliosi, who was the prosecuting attorney in the Manson Family murder trials, often discussed the importance of circumstantial evidence in the criminal justice system. He contrasted his personal view of circumstantial evidence with the commonly known "chain link" analogy. For many, circumstantial evidence is viewed as links of a chain, whereby, if a link is broken, the evidentiary strength of the entire chain collapses. Bugliosi took a different position and likened circumstantial evidence to the individual strands of a rope. He viewed each evidentiary fact or inference as a strand added to the rope, making it stronger. A broken strand may weaken the rope, but it will not necessarily break it.

As trained observers, police officers are tasked with finding those individual "strands of rope" in their investigations. They must allow the evidence to guide them, rather than dictate where that evidence should go. This approach helps officers avoid tunnel vision as they search for information and allows them to recognize preconceived notions.

So, What Is Actually Required for a Crime?

In general, for a crime, there must be a criminal statute or other defined law that declares an action illegal. A person must then perform that prohibited action, with the intention to do so. This is commonly referred to as the "mens rea" or intent requirement in criminal law. Usually, the person's completion of that prohibited action causes some type of injury, loss, or damage. However, there are some exceptions to this, such as when a person takes a substantial step towards attempting the prohibited action but fails to complete it.

In many instances, crimes are apparent, such as when there is direct evidence and the elements of the crime are basic. The officer who personally witnesses a violent assault will likely have little doubt about the presence or absence of criminal activity.

Other crimes, though, by their very nature, are more subtle, and require greater "digging" before criminal charges can be brought. These crimes are often uncovered through circumstantial evidence, and tend to be common with transactional, computer, or "paper-trail" crimes. Examples include crimes such as embezzlement, money laundering, or cybercrime. It is important that officers learn to identify when a crime has been committed, or at least be able to recognize when they need resources to assist them in making that determination. In other words, they must either have the answer or know where to find it.

Broadly speaking, the criminal justice system has many levels. Cases usually begin when police officers respond to calls for service. The initial investigations are closely intertwined with each stage of the process that follows. When a case moves through the justice system, it is reviewed at every level. For instance, police supervisors review reports for accuracy and correctness. Prosecutors screen cases for the strength of the evidence and likelihood of conviction. Defense attorneys scrutinize police investigations in every respect, with most seeking dismissals or other pretrial resolutions. If a case is brought to trial, the fact finder (judge or jury) weighs the evidence. If a criminal defendant is subsequently found guilty, an appeals court is usually asked to review the conviction.

Importantly, our legal system requires that each element of a crime be proven beyond a reasonable doubt. This is the highest standard of proof under the law. And, notably, it differs from the probable cause standard, which we know, is the threshold for a suspect's initial arrest. The product is that, before a case goes to trial, it will undergo much scrutiny. This usually starts with an examination of how criminal elements were established in a police report.

Although this may seem self-explanatory, there is much more to it. Think about it. If an officer seeks to charge a suspect with the theft of a cell phone, that officer must *confirm* that the cell phone was actually stolen. Evidence of a lost cell phone, without more, would be insufficient. If the theft is confirmed, the officer must also identify the *level* of the offense committed. Theft of highly valued items may be classified as a felony instead of a misdemeanor. So, in the end, every factual variation can impact a case in a very real way. With this in mind, let's take a more in depth look at an example of how an officer's deliberative processes may play out.

Hit and Run Example

You are working your patrol shift and receive a call to respond to a motor vehicle crash. The dispatcher tells you that the accident involves two vehicles. As you head to the scene, you mentally prepare yourself for the call by anticipating your duties in different scenarios. What if someone is injured? What if one of the drivers is intoxicated? What if the cars are causing traffic congestion? What if physical evidence needs to be preserved? Are there witnesses?

When you arrive on scene, you learn that the driver of one of the involved cars fled the scene. A witness described seeing a blue sedan, driven by a middle-aged male operator, "speed off" towards the Sunshine Apartments located to your west. According to the witness, the driver never exited his car.

- **From these facts, do you think that a criminal offense has been committed?**
- **If you are not sure, where could you look to find the answer?**
- **Do you have any thoughts about what your next step might be?**

Let's say that you broadcast the description of the suspect's vehicle to surrounding officers. You then get the scene under control and review your state's motor vehicle statutes. You determine that the fleeing driver likely committed a crime by failing to stop at the scene of the crash. The statute you located provides that:

- **The "hit and run" of an attended vehicle is prohibited. (Remember, if no law prohibits the action, there is no crime.)**
- **A motor vehicle crash must occur between two or more vehicles. Therefore, you must be able to demonstrate that the damage to the victim's car was *caused* by the crash with the suspect's vehicle (i.e., it was not pre-existing damage).**

- **The driver of the fleeing vehicle was *knowingly* involved in the crash and *intentionally* fled the scene; and**
- **The fleeing operator *made no attempt* at or near the scene to contact police to report the crash.**

These are basic crime elements that can be established through factual determinations and reasonable inferences. For example, by using your five senses, you could quickly identify information that reveals the damage to the victim's vehicle was not pre-existing. There may be broken glass or leaked fluid at the scene that is easily connected to the struck vehicle, or you may smell the burnt odor of a deployed airbag or see it deflated on the driver's seat.

Keeping with this scenario, how could you demonstrate the driver was *knowingly* involved in the crash and *intentionally* fled the scene? Questions like this seem odd, but they are the basis of many common defenses. Suppose that due to the large size of the "fleeing" operator's vehicle or the minimal damage it sustained, the driver was unaware of the collision. What if the operator simply pulled into a nearby parking lot for safety but did not have a cell phone to call the police? The takeaway here is that subtle factual variations can have significant impacts on a case, so there is an ongoing need to be thorough in your investigations.

Many times, a suspect's criminal intent can be implied through their *later* actions. A person's behaviors following an event may reveal their "consciousness of guilt", which is powerful circumstantial evidence. Examples could be the suspect's later attempt to conceal the vehicle under a tarp, or his attempt to prevent a witness from providing a written statement to police.

As the investigator, there are a wide range of questions that could be helpful in solving this case and then properly documenting it. For instance:

- **Was there debris left behind by the fleeing vehicle that could assist in identifying the car's make, model, or color?**
- **Were there skid marks that could indicate the unknown vehicle's tire size?**
- **Were there surveillance cameras that captured footage of the crash or the vehicle as it left the scene?**
- **Did any witnesses obtain the registration plate of the fleeing vehicle? Even a partial plate or state of origin will be helpful.**

- **Did the fleeing driver sustain injuries in the crash? In more serious cases, an officer may attempt to follow up with the local hospital to see if anyone sought treatment.**

Winding down with this scenario, this case would likely result in two distinct, but associated reports. First, there would be an accident report describing the crash scene investigation. Second, if that investigation established sufficient probable cause to believe that the "fleeing" driver violated the hit and run statute, there would be an associated arrest report when the suspect was located and formally charged.

If you are finding this process a little confusing, you are not alone. Most officers beginning their careers must learn to work through the many nuances of criminal investigations. In everyday policing, this process can be tricky, demanding, and even frustrating. The way that cases are organized and then carried out, especially complex ones, will directly impact their success. Remembering to outline how each element of a crime was met is a big first step.

A Word on Supplemental Report Narratives

Supplemental reports do not occupy their own category of reports. They are extensions of the original report, regardless of the type. Supplemental reports typically fall into one of two types: those completed by the primary officer and those completed by officers assisting in an investigation. When the primary officer completes a supplemental report, it is usually to include information learned after the initial report was submitted. Assisting officers, on the other hand, usually write supplemental reports to document their involvement in a case. For instance, they may be present at the initial scene or may be tapped to conduct follow-up work.

When completing a supplemental narrative, officers must remember to refer the reader back to the main report. The facts and circumstances that gave rise to the investigation in the first place will often provide some legal justifications for the actions they are now taking. Here are some examples of why an officer may write a supplemental narrative.

- **After an incident report is written, a suspect is identified.**
- **A victim identifies additional items stolen from their home after reporting a burglary.**
- **The weapon used in a crime is later found.**
- **A witness to a crime or event comes forward to give a statement.**
- **A detective follows up on a case.**
- **A new officer is assigned to a case.**
- **A previously stolen vehicle is recovered in another state.**
- **A missing person is located during a traffic stop.**

This list could occupy its own book. The main takeaway is that investigative information is wide-ranging, and as a case evolves, all relevant information must be documented.

Summary

You have probably formed the impression that the criminal justice field is not an exact science. Instead, it is a discipline peppered with situations that require judgment calls and decisiveness. The result is that officers must develop a reliable compass to exercise their discretion and report what they learn.

Common police reports taken at the patrol level are usually categorized into one of the following categories: **Case Reports** (or Crime Reports, Incident Reports, or Offense Reports), **Accident Reports** (or Crash Reports), **Arrest Reports**, and **Field Interview Reports** (or Field Investigation Reports or "Stop and Chats"). All serve very distinct purposes, but due to the fluid nature of policing, there are times when officers must document the same event with more than one report type.

When multiple reports are needed for an individual case, it is very important that each report reference the other. This provides the reader with key information to understand the moving parts of an investigation. At the same time, it illustrates the specific investigative duties of those who assisted in the case. Your agency's policies and practices will guide you here.

When writing an arrest report, you must ensure that the evidence uncovered during an investigation meets the necessary elements of the criminal offense charged. Arrest cases deal directly with a person's liberty, so relevant information that establishes the connection between offense and offender must be clearly articulated. Minor factual variations can have major impacts on a case, so attention to detail in your report must always be a priority.

Chapter 7
A Quick Stroll Through the Weeds: Documenting Constitutional Requirements in Police Reports

Each person involved in a criminal investigation is entitled to several constitutional protections. In the eyes of the law, these legal protections are considered indispensable. In fact, the failure to honor a person's constitutional rights can have a catastrophic impact on a criminal case, irrespective of a suspect's guilt. The notion that society's respect for the law starts with those who enforce it remains a cornerstone of modern-day policing.

The constitutional protections triggered by a criminal investigation stem from the unique role of self-government. And since officers are members of the executive branch, the rules of criminal procedure act as a "check and balance" against governmental intrusion. In our republic, any interference with a person's personal freedoms must be legally justified and non-arbitrary. Importantly, someone need not be a suspect or a defendant for these protections to be triggered.

Depending on the stage of an investigation, or the nature of the investigation itself, certain rights may be applicable. For instance, the Sixth Amendment's right to counsel pertains to those formally charged with a crime, while the Fourth Amendment protects against unreasonable searches or seizures, regardless of whether a criminal complaint has been filed.

Police officers must have a firm grasp of the procedural requirements triggered by an investigation. It is likely that many of these requirements have been covered during your academy training or criminal justice courses. Given the inherent complexity of the government's use of its own power, there are large bodies of law resolving questions raised during the criminal justice process.

Case law provides analysis of factual distinctions, defines legal exceptions as they are carved out, and probes where specific issues may become interwoven with other areas of law. An officer should understand, for example, that the right to free speech through expressive conduct originates in the First Amendment, while a defendant's right to confront adverse witnesses is found within the Sixth Amendment. An officer must know the difference between reasonable suspicion and probable cause and how each legal standard impacts a person's personal freedoms.

For the purposes of this book, we need not explore the intricacies of American criminal procedure. That endeavor is beyond our needs. Rather, the intention of this chapter is to underscore how vital it is for officers to be detailed in documenting *when* and *how* they honored a person's constitutional rights.

This is not an aspect of an officer's duties that can be overlooked. If we know that reports are the embodiment of an investigation, then the investigation itself *must always conform to the law*. There is no other way. Beyond ensuring that people have a reasonable opportunity to exercise their constitutional rights, police officers must be diligent in documenting *how and when they provide those opportunities*. If there is any indication that a constitutional protection was neglected, the case associated with it will likely be dismissed. In some instances, if the severity of the constitutional violation is sufficiently egregious, the officer could be subjected to disciplinary action, civil liability, or criminal sanctions. These are repercussions that are regrettable and entirely avoidable.

Custodial Interrogation Example

Every time an officer conducts a custodial interrogation, several constitutional safeguards are triggered. Most notably, suspects and defendants have the right to remain silent and cannot be compelled to speak with police. If they voluntarily choose to talk to the police, they can elect to have a lawyer present during questioning. This would be at no cost to them if they are unable to afford legal representation.

These rights are found in the Fifth and Sixth Amendments to the Constitution. In a technical sense, these amendments are quite different, but both have the purpose of ensuring that a criminal suspect's statements are not coerced.

As an investigative tool, custodial interrogations are widely used by members of law enforcement. Skilled interrogators can be effective in eliciting confessions or inculpatory statements from an accused, and these hold significant evidentiary value. In fact, the impact that an incriminating statement can have on a defendant can be significant, so interrogations are frequently challenged by defense attorneys. Many times, challenges come from the circumstances surrounding the interrogation process itself rather than the statements made. For instance, an attorney may argue that a statement was involuntary, or that there were no Miranda warnings given prior to questioning. These challenges stem from the procedural reality that suppressed statements generally cannot be introduced in court without the application of a legal exception.

With custodial interrogations, the investigator usually has a reasonable belief that the subject of the questioning was involved in a crime. To qualify as a custodial interrogation, the target must be in police custody while being probed for incriminating information. Both prongs must be present – custody and incriminating questions. Ultimately, the goal of a custodial interrogation is to identify information that either directly or indirectly connects the suspect or defendant to the crime being investigated.

Comparatively, a basic interview differs from a custodial interrogation. Interviews are typically less confrontational and tend to lack the formality and intensity of an interrogation. Although interview subjects can be criminal suspects, their presence at the interview remains entirely voluntary. In other words, unlike a person undergoing a custodial interrogation, interviewees are *free to leave*. The result is that an officer's approach tends to be softer. While interviews can still be intrusive and share the goal of obtaining material information, they are typically less exacting on the person who is being questioned.

Although the targets of custodial interrogations are technically in custody, they need not have been formally charged with a crime. Barring a legally recognized exception, statements taken in violation of the Fifth or Sixth Amendments will be suppressed. To be admissible in court, incriminating statements must have been made freely, knowingly, and voluntarily.

The failure to provide suspects or defendants with notice of their rights is both a critical and compounding error. For example, evidence that is uncovered as a result of the incriminating statement is usually suppressed as well.

Our rule of law deeply values personal liberty. Strict adherence to the United States Constitution is paramount in our criminal justice system. You will see that courts are cautious in their approach to legal challenges in these areas. One important reason for judicial prudence is to encourage law enforcement members to be diligent in meeting their legal responsibilities.

When defendants or suspects initially waive a constitutional right, such as the right to counsel, they can still later assert it. In this way, their waiver does not operate as a permanent decision or an absolute bar. For example, the subject of an interrogation may initially be cooperative and answer questions.

However, if during the interrogation the subject has a change of heart, they can invoke their right to remain silent at any time.

When officers are mindful of the scrutiny later applied by courts, they are better able to recognize the specific details needed in their reports. Legal holdings on constitutional issues are highly consequential. Therefore, officers are well-served by improving their understanding of the nuances of criminal procedure.

Let's look at a case that involves the issuance of Miranda warnings. Imagine that our suspect, Peterson, is interrogated by Officer Adams after he received credible information that Peterson was involved in a drive-by shooting. From the following narrative excerpt, do you think that the Officer Adams narrative is complete?

After Peterson sat down in the holding room, I advised him of his rights. I then asked him if he was involved in the drive-by shooting at the Elm Road Memorial Park. He said that he was, but it was self-defense.

This narrative excerpt is deficient for several reasons. Can you identify why?

For starters, it lacks detail and creates more questions than answers. If charges were later filed against Peterson, an astute defense attorney could capitalize on the limited information the narrative provides. Likewise, a prosecutor might be hesitant to take this case to trial. Here are some of the glaring questions it creates:

- **Did Peterson respond to the police station voluntarily or was he brought there against his will?**
- **If Peterson went to the police station voluntarily, was he free to leave?**
- ***What* were the rights that was Peterson given?**
- **Did Officer Adams recite "the rights" from memory or were they read to Peterson from a prepared form?**
- **Did Peterson make any incriminating statements to Officer Adams *before* he was advised of his rights?**
- **Did Peterson understand his rights? If so, how can you tell?**

- If Peterson waived any of his rights, did he do so freely, knowingly, and voluntarily?
- Was Peterson aware of the crime he was suspected of committing?
- If a rights form was provided to him, was Peterson given the opportunity to review that form? Did he sign it?
- Did Peterson request legal representation?
- Was the interrogation recorded?

These are very real questions. If Peterson confessed to the crime, but later recanted his confession, the brief report excerpt above would create problems for the prosecution. For instance, if Peterson testified at trial that he was not advised of his rights, or that he did not understand them, how would Officer Adams be able to combat this? Notice here that these questions are not ones of innocence, but rather ones of procedure.

The best way to combat defense challenges to an investigation is with information. Describing events as they occur is a start, but officers should also be mindful of any legal requirements that apply. Here, we know that a custodial interrogation means the person of interest is (1) not free to leave and is (2) asked questions designed to elicit incriminating information. Including the specific details on how these duties were met will later be of great interest to a judge or jury. Consider this more detailed excerpt of the case involving Peterson:

I escorted Peterson into holding room #1 of the Westerfield Police Department. This area is equipped with audio and video recording capabilities. I verified that the equipment was functioning properly and advised Peterson that he would be recorded.

Peterson took a seat at the conference table. I explained to him that he was the primary suspect in a drive-by shooting that occurred at Elmwood Memorial Park on February 7, 2022. I advised Peterson of his Miranda rights by reading them to him verbatim from a preprinted Westerfield Police Department rights form.

Next, I requested that Peterson read the form himself. Once he was finished reviewing the form, he stated that he understood his rights

and signed the form. Peterson placed his signature on the form at 2347 hours. He did not request an attorney.

I asked Peterson if he was involved in the drive-by shooting at the Elmwood Memorial Park. Peterson responded that he was, but that he was acting in self-defense. He then provided me with the following information.

And so on.

This narrative provides much more detail about the custodial interrogation. The officer did not coerce Peterson or attempt to overbear his will. Importantly, before any questions were even asked of him, Peterson was afforded the opportunity to review and sign the rights form. Likewise, the entire meeting was audio and video recorded. These factors support the view that Peterson freely, knowingly, and voluntarily waived his rights before providing the officer with incriminating information.

Under these circumstances, Peterson's statements would generally be admissible in court. Peterson behaved in a way that evidenced his willingness to speak with the officer about the event, most notably through his assertion that his actions were in self-defense. His attempt to justify his actions also helped to directly connect him to the shooting. Moreover, if Peterson later recanted his statements, the recordings could be introduced, and coupled with the other factors here, there would likely be enough evidence to prove a voluntary waiver of his rights.

"Constitutional" – A Word That Means Something

Like other professions, law enforcement has a requisite standard of care. We can ask, "Would a 'reasonable and prudent' police officer, in the same or similar circumstances, have acted in a similar way?" By answering this question, we can measure an officer's actions against those that are commonly accepted within the profession.

In a very real sense, an officer's lack of awareness of a legal rule or procedure is not enough to stave off a defense challenge. In the criminal justice system, *ignorance of the law does not justify a deviation from it.*

Each day, members of law enforcement deal with a variety of constitutional rules that form the basis of criminal procedure. At a minimum, officers should have a basic understanding of those commonly encountered. This would include not only the specific rule or standard, but its recognized exceptions as well. Here is a sampling:

- **Search and seizure under the Fourth Amendment.**
- **The probable cause standard.**
- **Exceptions to the warrant requirement.**
- **The rights afforded to an accused under the Fifth and Sixth Amendments.**
- **Rules for temporary detentions.**
- **Conditions of prisoner release, such as the right to arraignment, bail considerations, and when release without a hearing is appropriate.**
- **The use of confidential informants.**
- **Unlawful expressive conduct under the First Amendment.**

Summary

This chapter is a shallow dive into some of the common topics found in a basic criminal procedure course. It is intended to get you thinking about the many rules and standards that apply to a police officer's job. Continuous training in this area is essential for staying up to date with an ever-evolving legal landscape in law enforcement.

A solid understanding of criminal procedure is an important first step for success in documenting criminal investigations. Officers who are cognizant of their legal responsibilities are better equipped to act in accordance with the law. In practice, this leads to criminal cases that are much more successful. Remember, the stakes are high when a case has a direct impact on a person's liberty.

Chapter 8
The Face Sheet

Police reports have two primary parts: the narrative portion and the face sheet. Each serves a particular purpose. The bulk of this book is devoted to the narrative section because the writing process takes practice. In this chapter, we will shift gears and take a closer look at the face sheet portion of police reports. As you will see, this piece of the report puzzle presents a helpful tool for synthesizing information.

We discussed in Chapter 4 that the narrative portion of a police report provides the reader with the "story" of an event. By their very nature, narratives walk the reader down an investigative path. This is not the case with the report's face sheet. There, information is organized into separate categories to create a digestible *snapshot* for the reader.

Most police departments utilize some form of computer software to maintain and process their police records. This software is generally referred to as a "Records Management System," or RMS. While these systems house vast quantities of information, they also provide mechanisms for researching and organizing the information entered each day.

As officers input face sheet information, they are at the same time incorporating this information into their department's RMS. This becomes part of the data that can later be searched.

The practical uses of an RMS system are extensive. As repositories of historical and demographic information, RMS systems hold many categories of information, such as:

- **People (i.e., victims, suspects, witnesses, reporting persons).**
- **Property (i.e., stolen property, evidence, vehicles, found items).**
- **Geographical locations (i.e., municipal buildings, parks, schools, hospitals).**
- **Arrest and search warrant logs.**
- **Dispatch logs.**
- **Contact information for other departments, agencies, and facilities.**

- **Procedures for handling unique, significant, or special events (i.e., natural disasters, civil disturbances, VIP visits).**
- **Numbers of citations issued (i.e., traffic, ordinance, bylaw, parking).**
- **Missing persons status reports.**
- **Restraining or protective orders logs.**
- **Site cautions (i.e., dangerous conditions or hazardous locations).**
- **Trespass warning registry.**
- **Call histories.**
- **Associations (i.e., parental information, affiliations).**
- **Staff schedules and assignments.**

Increases in technology and upgraded reporting methods have resulted in more efficient ways of performing daily work. For instance, officers can complete reports by using mobile data terminals (MDT's), or they can explore RMS records in real time for investigative purposes. They can upload information to their department's database or electronically transmit case information to the court quickly and securely.

Data entry for a face sheet is usually done via drop-down menus or fillable sections. Once case information is input by the officer, it is viewable as a final face sheet that can be printed out and attached to the investigative file. Contrasted with a report narrative, which gives the reader a step-by-step account, the face sheet simply *lists* information. It is a preview of an event that can be easily digested before diving into the report narrative. For example, a typical face sheet will include:

- **A report number.**
- **The officer's name and rank.**
- **The date, time (or specified range), and location of the incident or event.**
- **The names of the people involved (i.e., victim, suspect, witness).**
- **Demographic and other identifying information of those involved, such as race, gender, date of birth, license number, and address.**
- **Event classifications or categories (i.e., vandalism complaint, domestic crime, protective custody).**
- **Booking information (i.e., mugshots, photographs of scars or tattoos, personal property inventories).**

- **Physical items, such as evidence, items seized, property recovered, and items determined to be stolen.**
- **Specific identifiers (i.e., registration plates, serial numbers, vehicle identification numbers, property values).**
- **Other information that can either be categorized or classified.**

ABC POLICE DEPARTMENT
123 Main Street
Anytown, USA 12345

Case # _______________
Officer Name _______________

EVENT

Nature of Crime or Incident _______________

Location _______________

Date Occurred _______________ Date Range (from) _______________ to _______________

Time Occurred _______________ Timeframe (from) _______________ to _______________

Statute (if applicable) _______________ Bylaw _______________ Ordinance _______________

PERSONAL INFORMATION

Name _______________ Date of Birth _______________ SS# _______________

Address _______________

Type (Check One): Victim ☐ Witness ☐ Reporting Party ☐ Other _______________

Phone (Cell) _______________ Phone (Work) _______________ Email _______________

Injuries (if applicable) _______________ Transported to _______________

SUSPECT INFORMATION

Name _______________ Date of Birth _______________

Address _______________

Phone (Cell) _______________ Phone (Work) _______________ Email _______________

Height _______________ Weight _______________ Eye Color _______________ Hair Color _______________ Gender _______________

Ethnicity _______________ Juvenile (Y/N) _______________ Parent Name _______________

Tattoos/Scars _______________ Clothing Description _______________

Suspect Condition: Alcohol ☐ Drugs ☐ Mental Illness ☐ Other _______________

M.O. Factors _______________

Year _________ Make/Model _________________________ Color _________ Style _________

Registration State _________ Registration # _________________________ Value _________

VIN _________________________ Towing location (if applicable) _________________________

Owner Name _________________________ Date of Birth _________ SS# _________________________

Address ____

PROPERTY / EVIDENCE #	PROPERTY DESCRIPTION	SERIAL NUMBER	MODEL NUMBER	VALUE	DATE RECOVERED

DRUG TYPE	SEIZED OR RECOVERED	TEST TYPE	WEIGHT	QUANTITY	DATE RECOVERED

Face Sheets as an Organizational Tool

Oftentimes, officers can utilize the face sheet to assist them in organizing their narrative. The indexed information provides key aspects of a case in an easily digestible form, such as the people, places, timeframes, charges, and items involved in a crime or event. In this way, a face sheet, can become a quick reference tool.

Here is an example:

You are on patrol and detain a person who is suspected of breaking into parked cars. During your pat down, you locate a knife in the suspect's right front jacket pocket. Due to its length, the knife is determined to be a prohibited concealed weapon. As a result, you seize the knife and arrest the suspect.

The typical face sheet will include a description of the knife since it was seized as evidence of a crime, along with any property numbers it was assigned. This data will be helpful for reference as you complete the narrative portion. Together, the face sheet and the narrative make up the bulk of the standard report. Here is how the knife seizure may look:.

Face Sheet Description: **Boning knife. Brown, handle, 4" blade, no discernable manufacturer information. Small crack near lower rivet. Valued at less than $10. Property number 12345.**

Narrative Description: **Jones was suspected of breaking into parked vehicles. When I asked him to remove his hands from his pocket, he refused. This caused me to fear for my safety. I placed Jones' hands behind his back with his fingers interlocked and I performed a protective pat down search of his outer clothing. While doing so, I felt a solid object in the right front pocket of his coat, which I immediately recognized as a knife handle.**

I retrieved the knife, which I identified as a boning knife with a brown handle. There was a small crack on the handle near the lower rivet and the manufacturer's information was not readable. I measured the knife blade with a standard ruler and determined that the blade was 4" in length from the tip of the blade to the heel. This classified the knife as a prohibited concealed weapon under general law 00-123.

I placed Jones in handcuffs that were double-locked and checked for tightness, and then transported him to 9th precinct headquarters. There, I photographed the knife using a standard ruler to provide

scale. I then placed the knife in a perforated cardboard evidence box. The knife was assigned property tag number 12345, which I affixed to the top of the evidence box. The knife was then submitted to the property officer for storage in the evidence room.

Summary

Face sheets are an indispensable part of a police report. They are a snapshot of information that represents the totality of known information at the time the report is written. Due to the ease with which the information can be viewed, face sheets are also an excellent tool for organizing and constructing a narrative.

New officers are encouraged to familiarize themselves with their agency's face sheet format early on in their field training. This will allow them to become accustomed to different categories of information required in a police report.

Chapter 9
Use of Force Reports

No type of police report garners more interest – and scrutiny – than a police use of force report. Although many situations can be resolved through de-escalation techniques or crisis negotiation skills, there are times when an officer's use of force is unavoidable. Under the law, the use of reasonable physical force is a necessary and proper exercise of an officer's authority when the totality of the circumstances dictates it. Most often, the use of physical force is prompted by behavior that threatens the safety of the officer or others.

Since use of force incidents can result in either injury or death, the reports that document them are *exceptionally* important. They must be specific and detailed. This means the circumstances leading up to the decision to use force, the use of force itself, and the measures that the officer took afterwards must be included. As we will discuss, the report narrative must describe the event *through the eyes of the officer*.

Police agencies will review *every* use of force incident. Additionally, an officer's use of force may be reviewed by other state or federal agencies, the media, or the courts. Can you think of some reasons why?

To determine what information a use of force report must include, let's start with the premise that *the use of physical force is legally justified in certain situations*. Officers can use force to protect themselves or others, up to and including deadly force. The key is for officers to recognize when physical force is lawful and when it is excessive. In doing so, they must also be able to quickly ascertain the appropriate level of force given the circumstances. Training and experience will always be critical parts of this equation. Put simply, though, force *cannot* be used to mete out punishment.

The goal of this chapter is to provide you with the tools to effectively describe a use of force incident in writing. Recognizing the information central to a force case is a crucial first step. Given that these types of situations are stressful and can quickly escalate, time and deliberation may not be an option. Regular training and mental preparation are necessary ingredients for achieving situational clarity.

In policing, the term *use of force* generally refers to those instances when an officer uses more than mere words to gain a person's compliance. This could be an officer's control of a person through physical skill or their use of an approved departmental tool such as a baton, O.C. spray, electronic control weapon, or firearm.

In this area, knowledge is power. The legal basis for an officer's ability to use force originates in society's recognition that some circumstances require that individual liberty yield to the need for public order. Oftentimes, officers must make split-second decisions on whether to turn to a tool or technique to gain a person's compliance. In fact, law enforcement members train extensively so that their instinctive responses to a stressful event comport with best practices.

When officers later write their report narratives, they must clearly articulate each fact and reasonable inference associated with the use of force. This includes their sensory observations coupled with any information relayed to them by others. With experience, officers can become adept at identifying certain behavioral cues that may escape the lay observer. To the trained eye, these critical signals become vital for their safety and the safety of others.

If no factual basis for force exists, the officers who use it will likely face consequences. It is as simple as that. Officers must always be mindful of the limits of their authority. The consequences of excessive force could be administrative sanctions, civil liability, or criminal charges. In the law enforcement world, use of force incidents are among the most litigated and costly for an agency.

Those who have faced allegations of excessive force – whether rightly or wrongly – must rely on their reports to defend their actions. This is especially true when no body-worn camera or dashcam footage is available. A typical case alleging excessive force can take many months to several years to reach a conclusion.

As a practical matter, reports provide officers with the opportunity to record facts nearly contemporaneously with an event. The result is that under the law of evidence, a report can be utilized to refresh an officer's recollection of the event at trial. The reasoning behind this process is that once officers recall the facts and circumstances they previously recorded, they will be able to testify from their own memory and negate any hearsay issues.

Remember that camera footage, while reliable, lacks the specific sensory experiences and internal perspectives of the officer. For instance, an officer's body camera may capture what is occurring in that camera's field of vision, but if the officer is looking to the side, the camera is not capturing the target of the officer's attention. This is a key consideration in the use of force equation.

When Is Force Justified?

It is not enough to report that physical force was needed to achieve a lawful goal. Although it may be a start, it falls far short of describing *why* force was needed and *how* the circumstances the officer faced justified its use. In policing, one of the most important cases decided in this area is *Graham v. Connor.* This is the seminal 1989 United States Supreme Court decision that discusses the legal parameters for police uses of force and the factors that courts will weigh during a review.

More specifically, in *Graham v. Connor*, the Supreme Court noted that an officer's use of force must be analyzed under the Fourth Amendment to the Constitution. Courts must apply a "reasonableness" standard since the Fourth Amendment prohibits unreasonable seizures. Under the law, a police officer's use of force is viewed as the seizure of a person. In *Graham v. Connor*, the Supreme Court initially noted that:

The 'reasonableness' of a particular use of force must be judged from the perspective of a reasonable officer on the scene, rather than with the 20/20 vision of hindsight...[t]he calculus of reasonableness must embody allowance for the fact that police officers are often forced to make split-second judgments – in circumstances that are tense, uncertain, and rapidly evolving – about the amount of force that is necessary in a particular situation.

As in other Fourth Amendment contexts, however, the 'reasonableness' inquiry in an excessive force case is an objective one: the question is whether the officers' actions are 'objectively reasonable' in light of the facts and circumstances confronting them, without regard to their underlying intent or motivation.

As you can see, when courts conduct a force review under *Graham v. Connor,* they look at the circumstances facing the officer at the time force was applied. Depending on the level of force used, this inquiry can be an intense one. In the end, though, a typical use of force case boils down to some basic questions:

- **How did the officer become involved?**
- **Did the suspect present a danger?**
- **Was the officer's response to the perceived threat objectively reasonable under the circumstances?**

With these questions in mind, let's take a closer look.

Officer Adams Encounters an Assault With Intent to Murder Suspect

Officer Adams receives responds to a call involving firearm. While in route, she is advised by the dispatcher that the suspect reportedly pointed a gun at another person.

When Officer Adams arrives at the scene, she sees the suspected vehicle speeding away. She notes that the driver closely matches the description of the suspect, so she conducts an investigatory car stop. As Officer Adams approaches the stopped car, she sees a pistol laying on the back seat. She immediately orders the driver to exit, but he refuses.

In this example, what should Officer Adams' next course of action be?

First, we know that the suspect is believed to be involved in a serious crime involving a weapon. This is bolstered by the presence of a pistol on the rear seat and his flight from the scene. Second, the suspect has demonstrated an overt act of noncompliance by refusing to exit the car. By his own actions, the suspect has escalated an already serious incident.

Before you move on, ask yourself what you would do given these circumstances. What is a reasonable response? What would be an excessive one? Would you disengage or retreat? Does the suspect's continued presence in the community create a public safety concern? Is an escalation of force appropriate here? If so, what level of force do you feel would be acceptable?

Moving on, here is what Officer Adams decides.

Officer Adams draws her firearm and continues to order the suspect out of the vehicle. He opens the door, exits, and quickly charges at her. Since she can see that his hands are empty, she holsters her firearm and quickly transfers to her electronic control weapon ("ECW"). When she discharges it, the suspect falls to the ground and she handcuffs him.

Was this use of force excessive or objectively reasonable? Is there additional information that you would like to know before making your decision? Would it matter to you if the suspect was injured? Why or why not?

These are just a sampling of the questions that will arise. Following a use of force, there is usually an internal review conducted, or in more significant cases, an external review by an outside law enforcement agency. Use of force cases will also generate much public interest, so community input is inevitable. This is especially the case when an incident involves social justice issues. Then, a police agency will typically receive information requests from media personnel, civilian review boards, individual citizens, and private organizations.

Moreover, in the wake of a high-level force case, such as an officer-involved shooting, most states require that the matter be reviewed by the local district attorney or attorney general's office. From there, some cases will be referred to the grand jury for review.

The comprehensiveness of a narrative will directly impact the layperson's view of an incident. To effectively describe why an officer's actions were objectively reasonable, the narrative *must place the reader in the officer's shoes*. Through their narratives, officers can demonstrate why their actions were appropriate and why the other alternatives were unsafe or undesirable.

Referring to our assault with intent to murder example, take a look at the following additional factors. You will note that each new piece of information builds upon the others. From your personal point of view, do you think that these factors are as compelling when viewed in isolation or in their totality? Also, as you consider each, think about which factor you find most compelling and why.

- **The dispatcher told Officer Adams that several witnesses said the suspect yelled, "I will kill you!"**
- **After Officer Adams stopped the suspect's vehicle, she observed that he started to fidget within the car.**
- **When the suspect was first asked to exit the car, he replied, "No way, I'm not going back to prison."**
- **Although Officer Adams requested backup, the closest patrol unit was more than five miles away.**

This should provide you with a clearer picture of why Officer Adams used force. Think about this situation from Officer Adams' point of view. Assault with intent to murder is a serious crime. The suspect was believed to be in possession of a weapon. She observed a pistol on the rear seat of the car. The suspect refused to comply with a lawful verbal command. His failure to exit the car and statements could be reasonably viewed as an officer safety threat. When he finally exited, he acted aggressively by charging at her. And so on.

While a firearm is considered a lethal tool, an officer's use of a CEW is characterized as a non-lethal force option. Both, of course, require extensive training. In cases where a CEW can be utilized, it has proven to be a very effective alternative. Given the circumstances, do you think a higher level of force *would have* been objectively reasonable? Why or why not?

Each new fact introduced changes the circumstances and greatly impacts an officer's response. It is good practice for new officers to get into the habit of thinking about the "what ifs" of a situation. This is a great exercise that helps officers mentally prepare for an event. What if, instead of a firearm, the suspect had a knife, brass knuckles, or no weapon at all? What if the suspect reached into the rear seat for the pistol? What if the suspect's windows were tinted, so there was no clear view into the car?

This discussion is not meant to stifle action or create apprehension. Swift decisions in the face of a threat are what keep officers safe. Rather, this discussion is designed to reinforce the importance of basing decisions on the totality of the circumstances.

Using a basic two-step approach, officers can take appropriate actions and then document those actions effectively. First, they must become familiar with their authority to ensure that they act in conformance with the law. Second, officers must consider the specific factors that impact their decisions. This will assist them in articulating why their actions were necessary and proper due to the information available to them *at the time*. Recall our premise that physical force is legally justified in certain circumstances. A good use of force report ensures the reader understands why the force used was justified.

Force Events When You Are a Witness

As an officer, you will also observe force situations involving other members of your department. Most agency policies require officers who witness a police use of force to complete a separate report narrative, regardless of whether they were personally involved. With the transformative nature of present-day policing, many states have even passed laws mandating that police officers intervene in any instance when they observe excessive force.

There are considerations that new officers may find helpful when facing a use of force event. What follows are that officers can consider in their decision-making process. By no means does this list account for every circumstance an officer might face, but it does touch upon the overriding questions that apply in many use of force cases. As an aside, these considerations can also be valuable for officers when they later organize their notes and write their reports.

What was is the nature of the incident?	• Serious crime? • Minor offense? • Non-criminal event?

Why is force necessary?	Is the person:
	• A danger to the officer or others?
	  ○ Combative?
	  ○ Assaultive?
	  ○ Predatory?
	  ○ Threatening?
	• Attempting to flee?
	  ○ Does escape create a risk to the community?
	  ○ If so, is that risk greater than the risk of acting?
	• A danger to themself?
	  ○ Threatening self-harm?
	  ○ Under the influence?
	  ○ Experiencing signs or symptoms of mental illness?
	  ○ Involved in a psychologically charged event?
	• Noncompliant or passively resistant?
	• Armed? If unarmed, is a weapon available?
	• Creating a disturbance?
	• Would force resolve the situation or incite others?

Some additional questions may include:	• Are backup units available? • Are there crossfire concerns? • What is the knowledge and skill of the officer? • What is the physical ability of the person?

Actions usually signal intentions. In some cases, this may be through a deliberate failure to comply or cooperate. Police officers will deal with suspects who seek to escape or attempt to cause others harm. They will encounter suspects who are provocative or who try to instill fear. Such actions, when viewed the through the lens of criminal behavior, can demonstrate "consciousness of guilt" or criminal intent. Here, the old saying, "Actions speak louder than words." is applicable.

Don't Label – Describe!

A police officer's narrative must not only label observed behaviors. Instead, it must describe those behaviors in a clear and coherent way. As you read police reports throughout your career, you will notice that some contain nonspecific or insignificant information. By and large, these narratives are ineffective.

Consider the following statements and think about each description. Which provides the reader with a better understanding of the reasons the officer used force?

Suspect's Actions *Labeled*	Suspect's Actions *Described*
1. Jones was confrontational.	1. Even though I ordered Jones to remain seated in his vehicle, he exited his car and walked towards my cruiser. While doing so, Jones clenched his fists and placed his arms in a fighting position.
2. Jones was argumentative.	2. Jones called me a "pig" and told me I was "useless." She then tore up the traffic citation that I issued to her and threw it on the ground.
3. Jones was combative.	3. Jones stared at me while he pulled up the sleeves of his sweatshirt. He then said that he would "not go quietly" and positioned his body in a bladed, fighting stance.

The "Safety" of Documenting

You may have heard the phrase at the police academy, "It is better to be judged by twelve than carried by six." The purpose of this saying, of course, is to underscore how important it is for law enforcement officers to be vigilant and safe. At the same time, this phrase does not account for the remarkable stress that a use of force event can have on an officer's wellness and psychological well-being.

The stress that follows a use of force, especially one that resulted in a person's injury or death, can be overwhelming for an officer. Make no mistake, these occurrences are harrowing in nature. It is not uncommon for an officer to experience painful feelings or other types of emotional distress in the wake of a use of force event. Even if the officer was not physically injured, they may suffer a wide range of emotional injuries, such as post-traumatic stress or survivor guilt. Depending on the severity of the event, the officer may temporarily be unable to return to work, and in more serious cases, may be placed on permanent medical leave or retired from duty.

To compound this strain, officers will experience legal processes resulting from the incident. For instance, they may be called to testify before a grand jury or may need to defend against a later civil suit. During each ensuing inquiry, the original use of force report will be dissected, examined, and scrutinized. The more clearly the officer describes the circumstances, the better the likelihood that the reader understands the reasons for the officer's actions.

Brady, Giglio and the Need for Truthful Reports – There Is No Other Option

It is starting to sound like an old refrain: police reports must be objective and accurate. They must provide a thorough and honest account of what happened. Likewise, officers cannot deliberately omit important information. In the eyes of the law, omissions can be construed as *affirmative misrepresentations*.

The cornerstone of a successful law enforcement career, and an officer's most potent weapon, is *integrity*. Without it, officers have diminished credibility and can be viewed as professionally ineffective. If an officer's integrity is called into question, the fallout can be disastrous. Beyond departmental discipline or decertification, officers can face criminal charges and potent legal challenges to their cases.

These impacts are based in large part on the cases of *Brady v. Maryland* (1963) and *United States v. Giglio* (1972). Officers with documented "integrity problems" can be portrayed to a judge or jury as untrustworthy. In essence, integrity issues sound a death knell for an officer's career.

Taken together, *Brady* and *Giglio* present prosecutors with certain legal obligations. When an officer has a substantiated instance of untruthfulness, such as deception in an internal investigation, that information is deemed relevant and potentially exculpatory. This translates into a mandatory disclosure of the information to criminal defendants.

Recall that under the Sixth Amendment, an accused has the right to confront adverse witnesses. Investigating officers are considered key criminal witnesses since their investigations are used to connect defendants to crimes. As you can imagine, officers with questionable integrity give the defense strong weaponry to impeach testimony or suppress critical information.

Summary

The reality of the public safety profession is that there are times when physical force is required. With each incident that results in a use of force report, though, the officer is presented with an opportunity to inform others. Officers can demonstrate how they did their job as they were trained. They can show why their actions were needed to protect themselves or others. They can describe the circumstances from their perspective and articulate how their actions were reasonable and lawful.

In policing, use of force reports are consequential, heavily scrutinized, and at times, politicized. There is no shortage of case law and public discourse that analyzes the bounds of police authority, and ongoing training in this area is vital. Under our system of justice, law enforcement officers can use physical force against another person, but only when the situation warrants it. The fundamental requirement is that an officer's use of physical force must be objectively reasonable under the circumstances.

Chapter 10
Taking Field Notes

During an average shift, it is not uncommon for officers to respond to calls of varying complexity. That means they must be able to shift gears quickly and gather information effectively. When call volume is heavy, officers may need to respond from one scene to the next without delay. This means that they may not be able to immediately write their reports.

As a result, field notes become an indispensable tool for officers. They serve as a memory aid. They provide a snapshot in time. They are the tool that allows officers to quickly document vital information.

This is not meant to imply that the only purpose of field notes is for later use in a police report. This is not the case. Plenty of times, an officer may record field notes when no official police report is required. Sometimes, these notes are taken by the officer for reference material. Other times, notes may be taken in anticipation of an event, or to share information with other officers or investigators. Our focus here, though, will be those field notes taken to assist officers with writing their narratives.

A helpful way to think of field notes as they pertain to police reports is that they are the *fundamental components of a comprehensive and accurate police report*. Field notes are intended to capture information that could otherwise be forgotten or lost.

Think of your experiences in school. Do you recall how important it was, especially as classes became more complex, to take notes? You probably jotted down key information that would later act as your study guide. Field notes are similarly used. The difference is that instead of using the notes to study for an exam, you will use them to write your narrative.

The use of field notes reminds me of one attorney's courtroom approach to jury trials. When speaking to jurors, the attorney would encourage each member to take detailed notes and would quote an old Chinese proverb that stated, "The palest of ink is better than the best memory." The message for field notes is really the same.

Usually, field notes consist of the notetaker's mental impressions and personal observations. Aside from concrete information such as names, addresses, and physical descriptions, field notes commonly include circumstances observed, inferences made, and details provided by others. At times, they are used to describe temporary conditions of a scene, such as a footprint in melting snow or tire tracks in mud. Consequently, the availability of a notepad is critical and, as a general practice, officers should always carry one while on duty.

Field notes should also be dated with times noted. This information may become critical if later evidentiary connections are made. Likewise, general observations such as weather conditions, lighting, or a person's demeanor, should also be noted.

In taking notes, officers must ensure that the information is legible and organized. Legible here means that officers should be able to later read and comprehend what they write. And more importantly, the notes must be organized in a way that allows officers to effectively *classify* information as they uncover it. This can be a challenge, though, especially when an officer is confronted with a chaotic scene. But, as with everything, one's ability improves with practice.

Classifying information can begin with answering the "who, what, where, when, why, and how?" questions. Each answer may bring another question, but this overall process can yield a manageable approach. For instance, an officer may start with the question of "who?" and create a list of people associated with a case. The officer may note each person encountered at a scene, and next to each name, provide a classification for that person, such as witness, victim, suspect, and so on.

When conducting investigations, officers must make full use of their observational and analytical skills. With these skills employed, they may find that their field notes are more than adequate for their report. At times, field notes may even reveal important connections that only become visible when they are later reviewed.

The ability to identify relevant information starts with asking probing questions. Below are some examples of what you might consider in an investigation and how the data obtained can be categorized. In your review of these examples, be sure to ask yourself: (1) "Why am I responding to this call in the first place?" and (2) "What must I accomplish during my investigation?"

General Questions for Gathering Field Notes	
Where did the event occur?	<ul><li>Specific address or multiple locations?</li><li>Public or private place?</li><li>Indoors or outdoors?</li><li>Within a vehicle? If so, was the vehicle stationary or moving?</li></ul>
What are the conditions?	<ul><li>Daytime? Nighttime? Dusk? Dawn?</li><li>Natural or artificial light?</li><li>Raining? Windy? Icy? Foggy?</li><li>Is the scene chaotic or controlled?</li><li>Are surveillance cameras available?</li><li>Any odors present?</li></ul>
What did you hear?	<ul><li>Are there distinguishable sounds?</li><li>Did you hear any spontaneous statements?</li><li>Is there noise or commotion at a secondary scene?</li></ul>
When did the incident occur?	<ul><li>Date?</li><li>Did it occur at specific time or within a broader timeframe?</li><li>Is the incident in progress?</li></ul>
Who is involved?	<ul><li>Victim? Suspect? Witness? Reporting party?</li><li>Is everyone still present or did anyone leave?</li><li>Has someone been reported missing?</li><li>Has a previously missing person been found?</li><li>Are there any accomplices identified?</li></ul>
Physical characteristics?	<ul><li>Height?</li><li>Weight?</li><li>Complexion?</li><li>Approximate age?</li><li>Eye color?</li><li>Tattoos?</li><li>Clothing?</li><li>Race or ethnicity?</li><li>Gender?</li></ul>
Other observations of the scene?	<ul><li>Are items damaged or destroyed (i.e., broken glass, pry marks)?</li><li>Is the area ransacked or manipulated in any way?</li><li>Have items been stolen?</li><li>Is there evidence left behind (i.e., tools, weapons, footprints, bloodstains)?</li></ul>

General Questions for Gathering Field Notes	
Is anyone injured?	• Visible injuries or complaints of pain? • Does the incident involve a fatality? • Is medical attention needed? • Has anyone refused to be treated? • Did you photograph injuries?
What type of event are you investigating?	• Crime? • Incident? • Car crash?
What other important details are there?	• Item descriptions (i.e., serial or model numbers, property values, registration plate)? • Is the call related to other incidents or crimes? • Are there any trends noted? • Have there been previous calls involving the same people or locations? • Did you conduct a search? • Is a warrant needed or is there an exception to warrant requirement? • Are other agencies or organizations involved?
What is next?	• Follow-up with witnesses? • Review camera footage? • Canvass the area or conduct surveillance? • Request additional resources (i.e., canine, fire department, SWAT)?

Checklists

Another effective way of taking field notes is to use a predetermined checklist. Checklists can act as an investigative "GPS" for individual cases, thereby guiding officers as they navigate through. With complex investigations, checklists can give officers "an assist" with organizing reports. Notably, each checklist can be tailored to a specific type of investigation. It is not uncommon to see checklists for crimes such as burglary, homicide, motor vehicle theft, and those involving domestic violence.

As an example, look at the next table. This is a basic checklist that outlines an agency's process for field-testing drugs. We know that criminal charges for possession, distribution, or cultivation of illegal drugs can be substantial. Officers in the field will encounter people in possession of illegal substances (actual or suspected), and field testing is an investigative tool. Drug testing, however, has become increasingly dangerous due to the potency of some substances. There is a very real risk of secondary exposure to officers, and many agencies have adopted protocols for drug testing.

Field Testing Protocol Checklist For Narcotics

- **If an officer locates a suspected drug or narcotic, a patrol supervisor will immediately be notified.**
- **When the suspected substance can result in criminal charges, the supervisor may either (1) direct the officer to seize the substance or (2) notify detectives to process the scene and seize the drug evidence.**
- **All suspected substances will be photographed prior to testing.**
- **All department members will utilize nitrile gloves when handling suspected substances.**
- **All substances tested in the field that yield a positive result must be packaged in a plastic evidence bag or sealed container prior to being brought to police headquarters.**
- **Substances tested at police headquarters must be done in accordance with safety protocols established by the Department of Health. This includes (1) the use of personal protective equipment, (2) testing in a predesignated area, (3) the availability of Naloxone, and (4) the presence of a second department member.**
- **When substances are stored for evidentiary purposes, they must be packaged and labeled according to established evidence policy. If additional toxicology testing is required, a notation on the evidence form will be made.**
- **All members involved in the seizure and/ or testing of suspected substances will complete a supplemental narrative to the original investigative report.**

Safety, Safety and Safety!

Field notes are important, but they should not take priority over an officer's personal safety or the safety of others. In all cases, notes should be taken *only when it is safe to do so*. For instance, if an officer encounters a violent suspect, it will not be advisable for the officer to approach that suspect with a pen in hand.

Summary

Field notes can be viewed as another tool in an officer's toolbox. They serve many purposes, but most importantly, they act as a memory aid and provide a snapshot in time.

Without question, the ability to communicate information to others is a skill that every officer must master. It begins with asking sound investigative questions, but also includes becoming an active listener. In sum, the factfinding process is designed to yield information that will help advance an investigation. And while officers gather this data, they need to effectively document what they uncover. Field notes provide an easy way to record key information that will later be included in the report.

Chapter 11
Let's Tie This All Together!

As with any learned skill, time and repetition brings improvement. Throughout this book, we have seen that police reports, by their very nature, vary from the very basic to the very complex. Still, the approach to documenting an investigation remains the same, regardless of the intricacies of a case. Reports will be successful when they are organized, accurate, and thorough. Officers will be well-served by remembering to ask those critical "who, what, where, when, why, and how?" questions. If an answer to any one of those questions is unknown, they just need to explain why.

Unfortunately, poorly written police reports can have wide implications. They can adversely impact the outcomes of investigations, even exceptional ones. Each day, cases are pleaded down to less serious offenses, or dismissed outright, when reports are substandard. This can be frustrating for officers and difficult for crime victims, especially when investigations fail due to legal technicalities rather than a suspect's innocence. In more serious cases, officers can face discipline, criminal or civil liability, and reputational harm.

Conversely, a poor investigation cannot take refuge behind a well-written narrative. When an investigation is shoddy, its defects are easy to expose regardless of the eloquence of the police report. Good reports are based on good investigations, and good investigations are successful when they are reduced to good reports. They must be compatible. This is why we have spent considerable time on the importance of sound investigations in this book. *The way an officer handles a case directly impacts the report that follows.*

Police reports also demonstrate to others how officers have done their job. They describe how officers fulfilled their duties, adhered to legal mandates, and navigated through an investigation.

New officers should become familiar with their department's policies on reporting. Similarly, they should identify some of the resources available to them and seek guidance from their supervisors. Initially, police recruits will practice report writing at the police academy. Then, as new officers, they will have their reports reviewed daily during their department's field training program. These collective experiences will give them the opportunity to expand their knowledge base.

In all, members of the law enforcement field are vested with tremendous responsibilities. They are keepers of the peace, enforcers of the law, investigators, and community helpers. The impetus for the shift from "warrior to guardian" is arguably due, in part, to the many duties that are now placed on police officers.

By the nature of their position, officers must be effective in many roles while generally working independently. In my experience, I have learned that the most capable officers are those who are inquisitive, but at the same time actively listen. They use their skills of observation in concert with their ability to analyze data. All the while, they work to determine what is important to a case, even when information is not readily apparent. In short, the most capable officers usually possess some investigative intuition.

As we have seen, police reports are a vehicle used to relay law enforcement information to others. It does not matter who is reading the report, what level of crime is being investigated, or the nature of the event that is being documented. Each report must be treated with the same care and concern. Remember that with limited exceptions, police reports are a permanent record.

As a way to continuously refine their substantive knowledge, police officers must make it a priority to regularly train. They must stay current with evolving issues in the law and understand the impacts of change on the policing profession and the criminal justice system. Since a police report is, in many instances, the most significant document in a case, it must be well-written. This starts with officers having confidence in themselves at a scene, and then in their ability to memorialize the information they learn.

It is my sincere hope that you have gained some useful strategies for writing comprehensive, accurate, and organized police reports. In the end, a high-quality product demonstrates that the officer is skilled, professional, and possesses integrity. These are attributes that exemplify an officer's commitment to the public good.

THE END